The
Accountable
LEADER

The
Accountable
LEADER

Dr. Costa S. Deir

International Leadership Seminars, Inc.
Lima, New York

Printed in the United States of America
INTERNATIONAL LEADERSHIP SEMINARS, Inc.
P.O. Box 56A
Lima, NY 14485
716-624-9660 (Tel)
716-624-9129 (Fax)

International Standard Book Number: 1-889433-01-2
Library of Congress Catalogue Card Number: 99-71805

*We dedicate this book to God
and His servants whom we
are called to serve.*

Acknowledgments

We are grateful for the help of the many who helped to make this book a reality. May the fruits of their labor be multiplied greatly for the glory of God.

Contents at a Glance

Table of Contents

	Numbers	Page

LIST OF STORIES

PREFACE

The Proverbial Concepts presented in this course of Leadership Principles will awaken the mind to receive truth. They are compacted capsules of truth for personal study.

Each focused statement is easy to understand, and by its brevity, prevents monotony in the learning process. It impacts, with rich variation, at times the emotions, at times the intellect. But above all, it moves the will toward greater Christian progress.

Each principle, by its illumination, directs the personality into brighter, healthier paths of living. They modify our ways of thinking, choosing, and acting, always aiming at excellence, always moving toward higher and higher levels of maturity in Christ.

The purpose of repetition of principles in different settings is geared to impact people at different levels in the process of maturing. The repetition will touch different planes of understanding through a variety of angles and approaches. This helps to drive the point, which carries the intended truth and purpose in view. This process is much like a carpenter who keeps on hammering the same nail until it reaches its destination safely and fulfills its purpose.

INTRODUCTION

Accountability is a vital part of life. It is not a commodity but an absolute necessity—like breathing. Accountability means willingly 1) submitting to the authority over us, 2) consenting to the scrutiny of our performance in responsibilities, 3) facing an evaluation that may reveal inconsistencies in our life, and 4) accepting just judgment when incurred by us.

Accountability activates our faculties. It challenges our potential to develop to its fullest—to perform perfectly and to fulfill our calling in life. Accountability spurs us to full commitment to be our best and perform the best with the highest quality and precision. It will always help us to keep the end in view.

Accountability awakens our conscience and every sleeping atom in us. Accountability carries with it the most serious state of agility. It keeps us always fully alert to perform with maximum effort, sparing nothing, while traveling on the road of excellence. Accountability demands that we be quick to observe and ready to move toward arising needs in the sphere of our responsibilities.

Accountability is the greatest saving factor from negligence, a light spirit, procrastination, lethargy, habitual forgetfulness, willful ignorance, sloppiness, poverty of purpose, and all mischief, and it saves us from running wild and giving vent to uncontrolled desires and undisciplined lusts.

Finally, *accountability prepares us to face God with overwhelming joy*, without fear and trembling, at the judgment seat of Christ. Nothing is more terrifying in life than to dismiss our accountability for the sake of the pleasure of the moment and deliberately ignore the consequences. The Scriptures remind us: "Be sure your sin will find you out" (Numbers 32:23, nkjv); "For everyone, to whom much is given, from him much will be required" (Luke 12:48, nkjv); and "We must all appear before the judgment seat of Christ, that each one may receive the things done in the body, according to what he has done, whether good or bad." (2 Corinthians 5:10, nkjv)

There is no fleeing from accountability to God and man. Every performance in life demands accountability at its culmination. The greater our sense of accountability, the more we excel in productivity and the more we move to the height of excellence. A serious leader recognizes and accepts his accountability before God and man. Accountability teaches us to walk in the fear of the Lord.

Accountable leaders do not belong to the "Self-Greatness Club" who crush smaller people in order to appear greater, for they know the awesome consequences that would await them before the judgment seat of Christ.

I. The Need for Accountable Leaders

Emptiness precipitates a series of crises in life. Unmet needs create problems in several areas in the process of living. Needs must be attended to for life to continue in its normal course. It is natural to have needs, but it is also imperative to yield to the inner drives in search of adequate answers to meet those needs.

No operation will ever succeed without having conscientious leaders who regard their accountability as the key to their success. Where there is no accountability, life resembles wild animals in the jungle. There's no standard of wrong and right, no principles to follow, no laws by which to abide. What's mine is mine and what's yours is mine also. Force reigns and determines the extermination of the weak and the defenseless. Everything is up for grabs, self service, kill as many as you can, terrify as much as you want—until all you desire is surrendered to you.

Where there is no accountability chaos reigns and death prevails. **Order in life demands accountability to authority.** No one lives to himself except the selfish, the proud, and the rebellious who deprives himself from joyful and fruitful living by refusing to acknowledge a higher authority over him, whether divine or human. To be accountable, we must be submitted to an authority higher than ourselves.

Embezzler thinks he's above accountability

A leader who was an efficient organizer and highly qualified in his field was entrusted with a gigantic operation to produce a quality product, which was highly rated on the market. He subtly embezzled millions of dollars into his pocket in a way that went undetected for a long time.

When he was finally caught, he was confronted by his board of directors to explain his actions. His statement was, "I am above the board, therefore I am not obliged to give account to anyone."❑

It is a well-known fact that the easiest person to deceive is oneself—thinking we are superspecial, smarter than anyone else, and deserving of special treatment beyond everybody else, culminating in acting independently as super-superiors.

The *selfish* sees himself as owning everything. The *proud* sees himself as better than everybody and everything. The *rebellious* sees himself above everybody and above everything. When this **terrible, horrible trio of traits** is found in a leader he is doomed to utter failure, though he may be successful for a season.

Sin has the element of self-destruction in it. Flirtation with sin, being the bait of Satan for selfish gain, results in terrible consequences and degradation.

Public trust of a leader is a privilege to enjoy, an awesome responsibility to carry through, and a fearful accountability to face.

A leader who is true to:
- *God* regards his responsibility as a *holy obligation.*
- *himself* regards his responsibility *very seriously.*
- *others* regards his responsibility as *important.*
- *his enemies* regards his responsibility *very compelling.*

A. Leaders are accountable to God and man

Regardless of who we are or what we do, we are all accountable to someone at different stages of our lives. Ultimately we are all accountable to God.

Man learns he is responsible for his own sin

A young man was confronted with the claims of Christ. He angrily answered, "I don't want to be a Christian because I once stole from someone coming out of church and he mistreated me harshly." He was told, "Not everyone who goes to church is a born-again Christian, and not everyone who goes to a garage becomes a car. Above all, no one is going to give account for someone else's sin, but for his own." He realized his accountability to Christ and surrendered his life to Him.❏

He fooled the world but died alone

There was an avowed atheist named Darwin who propagated his belief far and wide with great boasting and pride of heart. He was very successful due to his prolific pen and eloquent words.

But on his deathbed his last words were most pathetic. As he was breathing his last breath, he exclaimed loudly, "I have fooled the world, but now I have to face God alone." His beautiful mansion where he printed his atheistic literature in the past is now owned by the Bible Society where Bibles are being printed for worldwide distribution.❏

Accountable leaders keep short accounts with God and man realizing the necessity of having and maintaining healthy relationships.

> **There is no fleeing from accountability.**

Principle	*Comment*
1. The most accountable people in the world are leaders, regardless of their level of responsibility.	• The more a leader is tested, the more he will be trusted. The more he is trusted, the more he will be entrusted.

Romans 13:1-7 (NKJV)   Let every soul be subject to the governing authorities. For there is no authority except from God, and the authorities that exist are appointed by God. {2} Therefore whoever resists the authority resists the ordinance of God, and those who resist will bring judgment on themselves....

2. The sum total of life is accountability to God and man, especially for those in a role of leadership.	• Every leader must always keep in mind his immediate need for accountability to man, and his ultimate accountability to God.

Acts 14:27 (NKJV)   Now when they [Paul and Barnabas] had come and gathered the church together, they reported all that God had done with them, and that He had opened the door of faith to the Gentiles.

B. Today's leaders are under close scrutiny

Due to failures of outstanding leaders in our generation, people have become more particular about whom they follow. This alert attitude should keep all leaders on their toes. People have every right to scrutinize their leaders to ensure their safe destination.

Hidden sin destroys a leader's life

It was noticed that a once very successful operation's profits were failing significantly. Upon thorough investigation by specialists appointed by the board, it was discovered that the president had embezzled huge amounts of money over a long period of time. The stress of hiding his wrongdoing caused this man, who once administered his duties efficiently, diligently, and with integrity of heart, to live on tranquilizers to calm his nerves and to be hospitalized periodically. This stress became so unbearable that he could no longer instruct and steer his subordinates properly or supervise the corporation. When the discoveries were made known he had a complete breakdown. Is there any wonder why his nervous system was a wreck?❏

Leaders who shun scrutiny are outright dishonest and fear being discovered.

Over 200 kinds of fear plague the human race. The most torturing fear is that of being discovered when not living up to God's standard. Constant fear drains nerve energy and leaves leaders nervous wrecks. Fear paralyzes a leader's faculties and renders him helpless and powerless to fulfill his mission in life.

It is far better to live with a continual sense of our accountability to God than to be plagued by fears that torture the soul and wreck the nerves.

Principle	*Comment*
3. Leaders are being scrutinized today far more than in the past, due to the episodes which have brought shame and degradation to the ministry. Conscientious leaders take their accountability seriously.	• People have the right to have godly leaders who live and perform in the presence of God. Anyone who occupies a place of leadership is in great danger, unless he is accountable and lives with an awareness of God's constant presence.

Acts 6:3 (NKJV)   "Therefore, brethren, seek out from among you seven men of good reputation, full of the Holy Spirit and wisdom, whom we may appoint over this business;"

Divine consciousness keeps a leader's…

- heart *pure*
- mind *alert*
- will *fully submissive*

II. The CHARACTERISTICS & SIGNS of an Accountable Leader

An accountable leader is...

- Alert...................... He performs with *agility*.
- Careful .... He performs with *the end in view*.
- Conscientious .... He performs with *uprightness*.
- Considerate .... He performs with *respect*.
- Consistent .... He performs with *inner stability*.
- Cooperative .... He performs *in unison*.
- Decisive .... He performs with *settled conviction*.
- Disciplined .... He performs with *precision*.
- Joyful .... He performs with *liberty*.
- Knowledgeable ..... He performs with *insight*.
- Loving .... He performs with *kindness*.
- Mature .... He performs *skillfully*.
- Mindful .... He performs with *thoughtfulness*.
- Progressive .... He performs with *vision*.
- Transparent .... He performs with *openness*.
- Wise .... He performs with *intelligence*.

Characteristics & Signs
A. In relationship to GOD

The root meaning of the word "relationship" is "entering one into the other." "He that is joined unto the Lord is one spirit" (1 Corinthians 6:17, kjv).

Every relationship with God and man has its own terms. We must relate to God according to His terms if we are to abide in Him and enjoy each other. Jesus said, "I always do those things that please Him" (John 8:29, nkjv). The Father said, "This is My beloved Son, in whom I am well pleased" (Matthew 17:5, nkjv).

Life rightly related to God has meaning, purpose, and destiny. Rather than barely existing, one lives vibrantly in harmony with God's purpose, in tune to His voice, sensitive to His leading, and prompt to do His bidding. This is living life more abundantly where the flow of His life is saturating and impregnating our lives, where His will has become supreme in our lives to live and to fulfill for time and throughout eternity.

Every relationship has its obligations and terms. Every relationship has its ultimate purpose for mutual satisfaction, pleasure, and fulfillment. In order to relate to God, we need to know what pleases Him in minute details, moment by moment. God has given to man a capacity and an ability to relate to Him on a personal basis that is most astounding in its quality, and profound in its meaning. What a privilege we always enjoy as we walk in wholehearted obedience to His revealed will.

Persecution draws leader closer to God

A leader who valued his relationship with God far beyond his life was confronted by the authorities in his country to either deny God or be sent to prison. He was sentenced to twenty-five years in prison in the coldest place in his country and ordered to walk about sixty miles in sixty degrees below zero weather. God helped him to miraculously survive the ordeal. God became more real, near, and dear to him with each day, as he enjoyed a depth of relationship that progressively birthed a fresh revelation of God in greater fullness. He won many to the Lord as God gave him favor.❑

God give us more leaders of such caliber in our generation. **A strong relationship with God is man's greatest privilege.**

1. Is responsible before God

Being a leader in God's Kingdom is the most awesome responsibility under heaven that anybody can assume and maintain. Daniel Webster was asked, "What is the most serious thought you have ever entertained in your life?" His emphatic answer was, "My individual responsibility to God."

Responsibility always culminates in accountability. We enjoy our privileges—we assume our responsibilities. We give full consideration to our accountability. This is life's normal process. Any violation along the way brings its just consequences.

He who carries through his responsibility rejoices greatly in the day of his accountability as it reveals his utmost diligence. He who assumes his responsibility faithfully is worthy indeed of trust. The reward of the trusted is being granted greater responsibility.

- To the same measure we assume responsibility, we please God and grow in greatness in His Kingdom.
- The faster that boys carry on their responsibilities, the faster they will become men of dignity.
- He who carries through his responsibility reaches new heights in God.
- He who fails to carry out his responsibility to its completion is a hindrance, blocking the progress of others.
- No one was born a failure. We become failures by choice not by birth or chance. Neither success nor failure is hereditary.
- He who carries his sack of wheat to the mill will have flour to make bread.
- Awareness of God's constant presence produces responsible men.

Responsible supervision makes a difference

A leader who was noted for practicing the presence of God was assigned the leadership of two failing operations in two cities. After accepting his new assignments, he revamped both operations. He put conscientious personnel in responsible positions and trained his people to be responsive and responsible under strict supervision. In a short period of time both operations proved successful and excelled.❏

A leader who carries his responsibility conscientiously will be backed by God and will be trusted by men. He will be able to accomplish great feats with precision that save time, money, and energy.

Principle	*Comment*
4. All leaders must remember that God is on the throne of the universe, and they are accountable to Him in their role.	• Accountability should teach us the fear of God and regard for authority over us wherever we assume our role.

Joshua 5:13-15 (NKJV)   And it came to pass, when Joshua was by Jericho, that he lifted his eyes and looked, and behold, a Man stood opposite him with His sword drawn in His hand. And Joshua...said to Him, "Are You for us or for our adversaries?" {14} So He said, "No, but as Commander of the army of the LORD I have now come." And Joshua fell on his face to the earth and worshipped...

Principle	*Comment*
5. The safest leaders to follow are those who meet God's standard of righteousness and holiness. They labor with their eyes fixed on the judgment seat of Christ, where accountability will be required in That Day.	• Living up to God's standard satisfies His heart's desire and releases His abundant blessings. When God's principles are joyfully and consistently applied, they meet His standards causing Him joy and satisfaction.

Psalms 119:11 (NKJV)   Your word I have hidden in my heart, that I might not sin against You!

---

6. Accountable leaders are ever conscious of the watchful eye of the Lord, wherever they are.	• They labor with consciousness of God's presence and are attentive to His voice.

Psalms 34:15 (NKJV)   The eyes of the LORD are on the righteous, and His ears are open to their cry.

Principle	*Comment*

7. An accountable leader lives in the fear of God all his life.

- Loving God helps us respect, esteem, and reverence Him highly.

Isaiah 55:9 (NKJV) "For as the heavens are higher than the earth, so are My ways higher than your ways, and My thoughts than your thoughts."

8. An accountable leader is the best teacher of the fear of the Lord. Wherever he goes, he is consistent in his ways.

- Walking in the fear of the Lord is walking with a consciousness of God's presence; which restrains leaders from doing evil.

Genesis 42:18 (NKJV) Then Joseph said to them the third day, "Do this and live, for I fear God:"

When a leader is rightly and consistently focused on the Lord he will produce quality work, which will determine his success. Leaders who live in the fear of the Lord fear no one else in life. They live uprightly.

a. [Is responsible] for all he has been given

Leaders who fulfill their responsibility grow up into full stature and accomplish great things that usher them into the hall of fame. To the same measure a leader has been trusted and entrusted, he is accountable.

Destroyed by a "little fox"
A successful leader greatly enjoyed God's blessings upon his life, without realizing that the greater the success the greater the temptations. One day he faced a temptation of an old weakness. While entertaining the offer, he said to himself, "I am doing fine, this one thing doesn't matter much." He woke up one day to discover that one thing was enough to destroy his success and plunge him into a state of no return. Never trust little foxes; they grow destructive, fast.❑

Alert leaders pay full attention to plucking any weeds that grow in their gardens. They discern the manifestation of any weak tendency and take immediate action against it.

	Principle	***Comment***

9.   Each leader is responsible before God for what God has entrusted to him, whether it be talents, abilities, vision, goals, objectives, strategies, or people.

- Our accountability is to the measure of our enlightenment and trust. Serious leaders take their accountability seriously. They perform diligently, swiftly, and circumspectly.

Luke 12:48 (NKJV)   "But he who did not know, yet committed things deserving of stripes, shall be beaten with few. For everyone to whom much is given, from him much will be required; and to whom much has been committed, of him they will ask the more."

10.   When a leader is destined by God for power and prominence, he must assume both a greater responsibility and accountability before Him.

- The greater our role, the more we must tremble before God and His word. With every privilege comes a responsibility and a comparable accountability.

Psalms 78:70-71 (NKJV)   He also chose David His servant, and took him from the sheepfolds; {71} from following the ewes that had young He brought him, to shepherd Jacob His people, and Israel His inheritance.

Principle	*Comment*
11. God calls every leader to accountability for each opportunity and ability He gives them to redeem and perform.	• Privileges carry with them awesome responsibilities, which must be constantly carried out with precision.

2 Corinthians 5:10 (NKJV)   For we must all appear before the judgment seat of Christ, that each one may receive the things done in the body, according to what he has done, whether good or bad.

b. [Is responsible] for all he does

Leaders who have been entrusted with much must maximize their efforts to accomplish much. Many great projects have failed because some of those who were involved failed to carry out their part, thinking that no one would ever find out.

Lack of individual responsibilities embarrasses church leadership

A story is told of a church that was surrounded by refugees who were deposed from their country. The pastor and elders agreed to buy a large empty barrel and put it in the foyer and exhort their people to each contribute a quart of milk to be poured in the barrel upon their arrival.

At the end of the church service the next Sunday, the pastor, elders, and people came to dedicate the milk before its distribution. After prayer, they asked the refugees to fill up their vessels with milk; to their shock and astonishment, only water came out of the faucet. When the pastor removed the lid, he discovered it was all water. It was a great embarrassment to say the least. None of the church members assumed his responsibility. Each thought, "If I bring a quart of water, no one will notice it."❏

Public failure is caused by failing individuals who don't take their responsibility seriously.

Subtlety leads to irresponsibility culminating in negligence and total breakdown. Irresponsible people specialize in creating excuses to justify themselves, only to hurt themselves the most. Irresponsibility produces cowards who stagnate in their growth and become a heavy burden on their family and society. They are escapists at large.

Principle	*Comment*
12. All leaders are in a position of responsibility and are accountable to God for their lives, behavior, and actions—they should always remember that "Above the high is the Highest."	• Developing a sense of accountability to God saves a leader from the destructive sins of pride, laziness, procrastination, and sloppiness. It causes him to perform accurately and diligently.

Proverbs 16:18 (NKJV)   Pride goes before destruction,
and a haughty spirit before a fall.

---

13. Since an accountable leader knows God keeps accurate records, he lives and performs circumspectly in His presence.	• Divine intimacy results in creating utter carefulness in behavior, as well as consistent performance. It creates a full awakening to respond fully.

Numbers 32:23 (NKJV)   "But if you do not do so, then
take note, you have sinned against the LORD; and be sure
your sin will find you out."

Great responsibilities carried through
as unto the Lord are the
"Gateway to Greatness" in His Kingdom.

Principle	*Comment*
14. No leader should think, say, or do anything he cannot ask God to bless, for God blesses only what He approves, what will glorify Him, and what will fulfill His eternal purpose.	• What originates from God always glorifies Him. It will be sustained by His grace and power leading to total fulfillment of His will and purpose. Hallelujah.

Genesis 4:4-5 (NKJV)   Abel also brought of the firstborn of his flock and of their fat. And the LORD respected Abel and his offering, {5} but He did not respect Cain and his offering. And Cain was very angry, and his countenance fell.

- Whom God **proves,** He *approves*
- Whom God **appoints,** He *anoints*
- Whom God **trusts,** He *entrusts*

2. Walks in Obedience
a. reports daily to the Throne

Leaders who see their desperate need for God and wholeheartedly seek Him every day will be loaded with His benefits (Psalm 68:19, nkjv). Headquarters for a soldier is where he reports daily for orders and fresh supplies. Ability without availability is fruitless.

Our availability to God reveals our willingness and readiness to move promptly at His bidding. That is what counts most in a life that is fully committed and wholeheartedly dedicated to God and His eternal cause on earth.

Reporting for duty

A guardian of a church noticed a man entering the church every day at noon. He would go straight to the altar, kneel down for about one minute, and then leave. The guardian became suspicious of him thinking he might be a thief wanting to steal some of the valuable icons.

One day he intercepted and questioned him in regard to his motives saying, "You don't kneel long enough to pray." He answered him by saying, "I see my daily need to report to the Heavenly Headquarters for orders. My earnest prayer is short, 'Lord, I am available to You.'"❑

Minutemen in large factories are trained to do everything skillfully. They report daily to the top manager and wait patiently for his precise instructions at any moment to replace anyone who may have had an accident and carry out their responsibility. Yet, they may do nothing for days, but they are always available. They are paid for their availability to use their ability when needed.

Our availability to God counts most in life, as we report to the throne daily.

Principle	*Comment*
15. The leader who reports daily to the throne of God for heart inspection and possible major surgery is safe, and safe to follow.	• He who takes care of his heart doesn't have to worry about anything else. Out of it will flow all the decisions of life, which determine his destiny.

Psalms 139:23-24 (NKJV)   Search me, O God, and know my heart; try me, and know my anxieties; {24} and see if there is any wicked way in me, and lead me in the way everlasting.

16. To be what he says he is, an accountable leader must accept the loving, yet strict, discipline of the Holy Spirit in his daily walk and talk with God.	• His only safety lies in his total submission to the Holy Spirit. In so doing, a leader will be safe in his guidance and enriched in his anointing and daily performance.

Hebrews 12:5-11 (NKJV)   ... "My son, do not despise the chastening of the LORD, nor be discouraged when you are rebuked by Him; {6} for whom the LORD loves He chastens, and scourges every son whom He receives." {7} If you endure chastening, God deals with you as with sons; for what son is there whom a father does not chasten? {8} But if you are without chastening, of which all have become partakers, then you are illegitimate and not sons. {9}...

b. lives in harmony with God's Word

Obeying God's Word shapes our lives into His likeness and thus satisfies His heart's desire.

Newspaper article changes criminal's life

A noted criminal was caught after many years in hiding and was thrust into prison in a special fortified cell. He was so dangerous, even the guard who brought him his food was being threatened and cursed daily.

At that time, a famous preacher was holding revival meetings in the city with great blessings flowing from the Lord. One day the leading newspaper published on the first page one of his sermons which was entitled, "What Must I Do to Get Saved?" When they brought the newspaper to the criminal and he saw the title, he became furious and crumpled it in his hands. Cursing he threw it on the floor. Having nothing to do however, several times during the day he would pick it up, smooth it, and read a portion and again crumple it.

Sometime in the late afternoon he managed to finish the article. He didn't know that God promised in His Word that "My word...shall not return to Me void." (Isaiah 55:11, nkjv). The Holy Spirit convicted and converted him. He was miraculously transformed. He asked for a Bible and he gave himself to studying it and began to manifest the fruit of the Spirit. Eventually he was entrusted as the treasurer of the prison. His testimony affected guards and prisoners and many came to the Lord.❑

When our life is lived in harmony with God's Word, it reflects His beauty. It attracts and draws many to Christ who will follow Him willingly and joyfully.

Principle	*Comment*

17. Accountable leaders live in harmony with God's Word, void of the contradiction that often exists between one's words and one's deeds.

- They speak what they first live. They experience the truth before they proclaim it. A leader who speaks out of fulfilled truth imparts life.

Matthew 7:24 (NKJV)   "Therefore whoever hears these sayings of Mine, and does them, I will liken him to a wise man who built his house on the rock:"

18. A noble leader always tests his life by a constant reference to the life, conduct, and teachings of Jesus Christ his Lord.

- Comparing our lives with Christ helps us come up to His standard. We must always aim at attaining God's ultimate and pleasing Him.

Philippians 2:5 (NKJV)   Let this mind be in you which was also in Christ Jesus,

19. When the Word of the Lord comes to a leader, he must respond to it.

- Every time God speaks there is a divine purpose to be fulfilled.

Isaiah 6:8 (NKJV)   Also I heard the voice of the Lord, saying: "Whom shall I send, and who will go for Us?" Then I said, "Here am I! Send me."

c. seeks God's light and guidance

A leader is safe as long as he sees his desperate need for God's revealed will to guide his footsteps in the path of His choosing. Only when we are guided by the Holy Spirit do we fulfill the will of God, and find fulfillment in life.

Lack of guidance causes downfall

A leader, having succeeded in the past, attempted a venture without divine consultation. It wasn't long before he plunged himself into a deep pit of great loss.❏

Every act independent from God causes us to miss His best, creating messes that grieve His heart, hurt us, and affect the lives of others. Past success does not guarantee present success, only divine guidance does.

Away with a life of guessing, imitating others, and moving out of presumption. That is dangerous living.

Principle	*Comment*
20. When God blows upon a leader's position, ministry, or finances, it is with the intention that he should seek the Lord for a fresh visitation from the Throne with humility of heart.	• Brokenness with repentance is the key that gets us back to God. When a leader does not respond to God's leadings, for whatever reason, he must expect God's dealings to correct his path.

Job 1:20 (NKJV)   Then Job arose, tore his robe, and shaved his head; and he fell to the ground and worshipped.

Principle	*Comment*
21. A sincere leader asks God to bring everything in his life to a climax in order to clear up and bring all hidden things into the light. What a deliverance!	• Honesty leads to openness, and openness leads to receptivity. Humility of heart leads to repentance, which is the gateway back to God and His forgiveness.

1 Chronicles 21:17 (NKJV)   And David said to God, "Was it not I who commanded the people to be numbered? I am the one who has sinned and done evil indeed; but these sheep, what have they done? Let Your hand, I pray, O LORD my God, be against me and my father's house, but not against Your people that they should be plagued."

---

22. An accountable leader is greatly encouraged by having God as his silent partner, who guides his life to perform his best.	• Partnership with God guarantees our success. Such cooperation ends all inner struggle and guarantees continual progress.

Psalms 121:1-2 (NKJV)   I will lift up my eyes to the hills; from whence comes my help? {2} My help comes from the Lord, Who made heaven and earth.

Characteristics & Signs
B. In relationship to OTHERS

We were created to relate to each other: to communicate, to interact, to give and receive, to share our lives with each other, to benefit from one another's input, to exchange our new discoveries in life, and the revelations that God entrusts to each one of us.

No one was created as a fully sufficient, independent entity to live by himself. Life's greatest revelation is to see our desperate need for God, and then for each other. We need each other more than we realize. When we share our needs it lessens our burdens, dissipates our unnecessary suffering, and encourages our hearts in pursuit of God's ultimate for our lives.

Life shared develops its potential and multiplies its joys. Life spurned shrinks into oblivion and ceases to exist. In our relationships with others it is imperative that we aim at mutual edification, regardless of the price each one of us has to pay. We need to see the need for each other, we need to meet the needs of each other, we need to look after the affairs of each other (Philippians 2:4), and we must welcome input and correction from one another when needed.

We need to be open to constructive criticism and scrutiny from each other. All those contributing factors are necessary for our maturing in character and performance. Our mutual respect for each other generates a receptivity to one another, resulting in mutual benefit, contributing to our progress.

To esteem each other above ourselves, is basic to flowing together in the pure stream of divine love, void of destructive selfishness that dissipates relationships and gives way to Satan to wreak havoc.

I need you

I was visiting one of our students who was working as a missionary in a foreign country. As I entered his office and sat down, something drew my attention, captivated my mind, and thrilled my heart. I saw a wooden plaque hanging on the wall with these words deeply engraved in it, **"I need you."**❏

Only three words, but its dynamic message greatly impacted me. If we but see our need for each other beyond the deception of our hearts and the independent spirit from which we suffer, we will begin to more easily relate to each other. It behooves us every time we communicate with God to verbalize these four words, "Lord, I need You." Likewise when we meet each other and depart from each other, after the usual greeting, to assure one another, "Brother, sister, I need you." Let's make ourselves available to God and each other.

Stranded

A man who had a flat tire discovered a defect in his jack. His frustration was compounded because he was in the middle of nowhere on a rarely traveled road. He waited patiently for many hours in burning hot weather in vain. At sunset he noticed a car coming from afar off. He stood in the middle of the road waving with his shirt. When the car stopped he cried with an exhausted voice, "I need your jack!" Within minutes, he was on his way thanking God for sending help.❏

Principle	*Comment*
23. A leader will be held accountable not only for his position but also for his disposition and the way he behaves toward others.	• The way we treat others reflects the measure of Christ that has been developed in us by His grace. The greater the maturity the better the treatment.

Colossians 3:17 (NKJV)   And whatever you do in word or deed, do all in the name of the Lord Jesus, giving thanks to God the Father through Him.

1. Welcomes scrutiny

When we know that we are facing scrutiny it helps us keep our heart pure, sincere, and honest in all that we think, say, and do.

Secret to well-behaved children

A father was asked, "How do you get your teenage children to behave so well?" His answer was a real revelation to his friend. "I told my children they are free to do anything they desire to do, if they promise to tell me the truth whenever I ask them a question. I stood by my promise and so did they. Ever since then we have had no trouble."❏

Honesty welcomes scrutiny under all circumstances. When we are honest with God we will be honest with ourselves and with others also.

The money to repair the house of the Lord during the reign of King Joash of Israel was handled by trusted men of whom the Bible says, *"Moreover they did not require an account from the men...for they dealt faithfully."* (2 Kings 12:15, nkjv)

- A leader proves his honesty by treating his people right.
- A leader proves his diligence by serving his people.
- A leader appreciates his people by praising them.
- A leader who admires his people's work will recompense them accordingly.

—No wonder he is greatly loved—

Principle	*Comment*

24. Accountable leaders welcome the scrutiny of those in authority over them, for it helps them walk circumspectly before God and man.

- He who welcomes scrutiny reveals the purity of his heart. No one is above scrutiny or above correction, except God Himself.

1 Peter 5:5 (NKJV)   Likewise you younger people, submit yourselves to your elders. Yes, all of you be submissive to one another, and be clothed with humility, for "God resists the proud, but gives grace to the humble."

25. Every leader has people who follow him and size him up in the process.

- Without people there would be no need for leaders who lead with loving care.

Exodus 3:10 (NKJV)   "Come now, therefore, and I will send you to Pharaoh that you may bring My people, the children of Israel, out of Egypt."

Principle	**Comment**
26. A wise leader measures his progress by the favorable reaction of his people, not by what he thinks.	• By his fruit a leader is known. Appearance can be deceiving, but fruit is the only genuine sure evidence.

1 Samuel 18:16 (NIV)   But all Israel and Judah loved David, because he led them in their campaigns.

- It is safe for a leader to be contented with what he has, yet it is dangerous to be contented with what he is.

- Leaders who can differentiate between their needs and their wants and are disciplined, will be safe.

- Leaders who are discontented with their accomplishments have discovered the secret of success.

a. knows he needs the input of mature leaders

Receiving the input of others can be a saving factor in a leader's life and ministry, and it enlivens his relationship with them. It is a fact that we need each other more than we realize.

Mature man of God mentors young minister

An independent young minister who acted on his whims violated several principles and came to the end of himself. In his desperation he realized his need for a mature man of God and came to the man weeping, crying, sobbing, confessing his violations, and asking for help. He received help beyond his expectation which encouraged his heart to rise and move with God, and to live in obedience to divine principles.❏

The right counsel of the mature is a great saving factor, while the wrong counsel kills like the wild poisonous mushroom. Regardless of how much humility is required to ask for wise advice, it is less costly than paying the price in hurtful humiliation of failure.

We cannot live by how we feel, think, or see things. Life is governed by laws and principles that must be highly regarded and wholeheartedly obeyed if we are to reap joyful results.

- Wise counsel is a great saving factor in a leader's life.
- A wise leader learns from the rich experiences of resourceful people.
- The immature leader learns only from his own experiences.
- The fool and the proud learn from nobody's experiences, all because of their self-sufficiency.

Principle	*Comment*
27. Every leader must be in relationship with mature leaders for his own safety and the safety of his whole operation.	• Healthy relationships produce healthy leaders and guarantee their growth and effectiveness in every realm of life.

Luke 10:17 (NKJV)   Then the seventy returned with joy, saying, "Lord, even the demons are subject to us in Your name."

---

28. A strong leader must be surrounded by men able to safeguard him and the whole operation with integrity.	• He who stands alone will, sooner or later, die alone. Isolation is Satan's deceptive way to quick destruction.

Acts 14:23 (NKJV)   So when they had appointed elders in every church, and prayed with fasting, they commended them to the Lord in whom they had believed.

Reprimanding evil without restraining evil is futile when the warning goes unheeded. Laws must be enforced without hesitancy or compromise.

Principle	*Comment*
29. Wise leaders plan their moves in cooperation with other leaders to ensure balance and safety, and to gain effective results.	• Wise counsel is a great saving factor. It must be sought after, greatly appreciated, and heeded seriously. There is no substitute for wisdom.

Proverbs 24:6 (NKJV)   For by wise counsel you will wage your own war, and in a multitude of counselors there is safety.

| 30. A leader who desires to get a truer picture of who he really is should consider the evaluation of others who are more mature. | • Proper evaluation demands utter honesty. Walking with God needs continual heart searching, honest judgment, and correction. |

1 Samuel 2:12,22-25 (NKJV)   Now the sons of Eli were corrupt; they did not know the LORD....{22} Now Eli was very old; and he heard everything his sons did to all Israel, and how they lay with the women who assembled at the door of the tabernacle of meeting. {23} So he said to them, "Why do you do such things? For I hear of your evil dealings from all the people. {24} No, my sons! For it is not a good report that I hear. You make the Lord's people transgress. {25}..."

b. receives advice

Many leaders' lives have been saved from disastrous ends due to their humble receptivity to wise advice. There is great advantage in heeding advice that is inspired by the Lord. He who heeds the advice of the wise will become wiser someday. The accumulation of wise counsel makes a leader resourceful enriching the lives of others to the same degree.

Warning to the Wise: There are those who take the advice of everybody and live in confusion, yet there are those who refuse to take advice from anyone and live in total isolation like a dry bone in a parched desert. There is safety in being discerning and balanced.

Not all mushrooms are healthy; some prove to be poisonous and destructive. So it is with taking advice without discerning the source, the motive, and where it leads. Advice given freely is seldom heeded. Costly advice is highly regarded and put to use.

Free advice is often unheeded advice

A multimillionaire had a problem that plagued him for years. Though it was humiliating to ask for advice, nevertheless due to his state of desperation he confided in his pastor. His pastor took the matter seriously before the Lord and then gave him the answer. The man kept coming back to the pastor for more advice, and the same advice was given each time, but it went unheeded.

One day the frustrated pastor confided in one of his members who was a psychologist who suggested that the pastor send the man to see him. The appointment was made, the psychologist listened attentively and gave him the same advice in psychological terms, charging him $2,500. The man implemented the advice and had great results. He phoned to thank the pastor for recommending the psychologist to him!❑

Advice unheeded is advice wasted. It takes crystallized wisdom to benefit from wise counsel. Many have lost everything for not heeding advice, and some have even lost their lives. In the business world, their motto is, "Never offer advice free, always sell it at a high price."

Principle	*Comment*
31. Accountable leaders should take advantage of all the advice they can get and benefit greatly from it.	• The more we learn the more skillful and productive we become, wherever we are.

2 Kings 22:13 (NKJV)   "Go, inquire of the LORD for me, for the people and for all Judah, concerning the words of this book that has been found; for great is the wrath of the LORD that is aroused against us, because our fathers have not obeyed the words of this book, to do according to all that is written concerning us."

32. A sensible leader desires to hear what he needs, not what he wants.	• Sincerity of heart makes a person realistic and practical.

2 Timothy 4:2-4 (NIV)   Preach the Word...{3} For the time will come when men will not put up with sound doctrine. Instead, to suit their own desires...{4} They will turn their ears away from the truth and turn aside to myths.

Principle	*Comment*

33. Every leader who desires to do the right thing and succeed according to God should get a second opinion from those who are more mature than he, regarding his lifestyle, the performance of his responsibilities, and his responsibility to his people.

- Progress demands that we take all the precautions possible and give serious consideration to the suggestions of the mature—who are rich in their experiences, hear from God daily, are updated regarding His agenda, and know the means and ways to perform adequately.

Proverbs 19:20 (NKJV)   Listen to counsel and receive instruction, that you may be wise in your latter days.

---

34. Every leader has blind spots and needs someone close to him to see for him and save him from possible pitfalls.

- We need one another to see for us more than we realize. Our receptivity to each other is a great saving factor.

Luke 10:1 (NKJV)   After these things the Lord appointed seventy others also, and sent them two by two before His face into every city and place where He Himself was about to go.

---

c. accepts criticism

Our attitude toward criticism determines whether we gain or lose the benefit that could be derived. Usually our response is determined by how we interpret what we go through.

To *reject* criticism is **foolish**

To *accept* criticism is **commendable**

To *resist* criticism is **unwise**

To *welcome* criticism is to **welcome progress**

To *ignore* criticism is **loss**

To *weigh* criticism is **beneficial**

To *neglect* criticism is to **hinder progress**

To *meditate* on criticism is to **extract its butter**

To *abhor* criticism is to **create a new enemy**

To *value* criticism is to **gain its benefit**

To be *indifferent* to criticism is to **neutralize its effect**

To *consider* criticism is **gain**

To be *hostile* to criticism is to **travel in reverse gear**

To be *favorable* to criticism is **enriching**

To *forget* criticism is to **bury a treasure**

To *react* to criticism is to **miss a great lesson**

When leaders react emotionally to criticism they usually miss the measure of truth that could be there. When they react intellectually, thinking only of themselves, they reveal the measure of hidden pride that always tends toward self-defense. When the reaction is most gracious, giving due consideration to the content, attitude, and the spirit by which it was given, much benefit is derived that can be the means to progress.

Dogs have a habit of barking at the new moon. The moon continues to shine bright and the dogs' criticism ceases when they lose their voice. This is the only way to treat destructive criticism.

Some ignore constructive criticism at a great loss that could have been of great help to them. The mature person benefits greatly from criticism and makes greater progress toward reaching his ultimate goal.

Criticism: easier to give than receive

A man asked a close friend saying, "Why is it easier to give criticism than to take it?" His answer was, "The more **proud** we are, the harder it is to take criticism. The more **selfish** we are, the more we fight criticism. The more **emotional** we are, the more we fear criticism. The more **immature** we are, the more we are insecure and tend to hide from criticism."❏

Principle	*Comment*
35. The leader who accepts criticism well and makes adjustments where it is appropriate is guaranteed to make progress.	• Just criticism, when accepted, can result in promotion to the heights of excellence affecting every area of life and its performance.

2 Corinthians 2:4 (NKJV) For out of much affliction and anguish of heart I wrote to you, with many tears, not that you should be grieved, but that you might know the love which I have so abundantly for you.

Principle	Comment

36. A wise leader knows that the tendency to be blind to his own faults should make him open to protests, suggestions, criticisms, and the advice of others, if he is to make any progress.

● Humility leads to receptivity. We determine the measure of our benefit by the measure of our openness. Pride closes a leader's heart toward God and man, and paralyzes his potential, at a great loss.

Proverbs 1:5 (NKJV)   A wise man will hear and increase learning, and a man of understanding will attain wise counsel,

---

37. The greatness of a leader is revealed by how he accepts or rejects criticism. Constructive criticism will inspire us to greater effectiveness in life.

● Insecure leaders are threatened by criticism, while mature leaders benefit from it, as they weigh it carefully and consider making any necessary changes.

Exodus 18:17-26 (NKJV)   So Moses' father-in-law said to him, "The thing that you do is not good. {18} Both you and these people who are with you will surely wear yourselves out. For this thing is too much for you; you are not able to perform it by yourself. {19} Listen...I will give you counsel, and God will be with you..."{20}...
{24} So Moses heeded the voice of his father-in-law and did all that he had said. {25}...

Principle	*Comment*

38. Accepting criticism can be the means of salvation from many unnecessary pitfalls, caused by pride, insecurity, immaturity, selfishness, and rebellion.

- He who welcomes criticism and mends his ways will live free from regrets. Regrets keep leaders under condemnation, which dampens their spirit.

Psalms 141:5 (KJV)   Let the righteous smite me; it shall be a kindness: and let him reprove me; it shall be an excellent oil, which shall not break my head: for yet my prayer also shall be in their calamities.

Destructive Criticism

Some leaders benefit from destructive criticism, while others are devastated by it.

Some criticism is destructive in content, some criticism is destructive in spirit, and some criticism is destructive in both.

Wise leaders glean the best out of the worst and gain insights that propel them forward.

Wholesome criticism is a great saving factor in life.

d. heeds objections

Only the wise heed objections and study carefully the intent, the content, and the reasons behind them. Weighing objections carefully and imbibing whatever benefit they offer is great gain.

Man heeds partner's objections and thrives

A heated debate between two business partners ended with an agreement to table the decision until the next day. The one who was very dogmatic and adamant that he was right and that the business must close for good could not sleep that night. He kept thinking deeply about his partner's difference of opinion which was diametrically opposed to his. Finally he saw some rays of light and with one adjustment consented. The business gained market acclaim and became very profitable.❏

Differences of opinion can be a means to marked progress when received and considered humbly and wisely. Objections resemble a large stop sign at a dead end that prevents us from falling into a deep river. Considering objections is very wise and prudent and a tremendous saving factor.

The fool listens only to those who tend to confirm his opinion and verify his prejudices. No wonder he is stuck in the mire of confusion with no hope of progress in sight.

For some people, their opinions stem out of their emotions; for others, out of their intellect; for others, out of their doubts and fears; while for others, their opinions are born by the Spirit of the Lord.

The wise gives full attention and respectful consideration to the opinions of others with as much weight as he does his own, and adds to himself extra wisdom that increases his intelligence and makes him wiser.

Principle	*Comment*
39. The leader who does not take heed to the objections of his followers will not have their cooperation in accomplishing his goal.	• Cooperation is the key to all accomplishment. No one can be a successful leader unless he has the full cooperation of followers who pledge allegiance to him.

1 Kings 12:16 (NKJV)   Now when all Israel saw that the king did not listen to them, the people...departed to their tents.

---

40. Accountable leaders welcome disagreements, give them due consideration, and derive all the benefits they can get from them and thus make progress.	• Seeing and considering the viewpoints of others can be the means to progress. It is the height of wisdom to heed the loving contributions of the wise, especially those who are richly experienced.

Acts 15:1-21 (NKJV)   ...{2} Therefore, when Paul and Barnabas had no small dissension and dispute with them, they determined that Paul and Barnabas and certain others of them should go up to Jerusalem, to the apostles and elders, about this question {3}...{6} Now the apostles and elders came together to consider this matter....

2. Is transparent

Transparency is the hallmark of Christian maturity. It delivers from all fears, it leads to a life of liberty in the Spirit that helps a leader function efficiently. Transparency before God leads to honesty before man.

Honesty develops transparency when leaders become fully aware of the presence of God. Honesty and truthfulness are sincere twins. Honesty pays double dividends due to its secret of lasting success. Many a person who seems to have an honest face does not have an honest heart to prove it. He who is not honest with himself will not be truthful to others.

Genuineness overcomes criticism

A transparent leader was criticized harshly and accused of being false. He continued to live genuinely and put all his critics to shame through his honesty, sincerity, and truthfulness, in his relationships and in his business dealings. His uprightness silenced his critics.❏

He that is honest glitters as a polished diamond. Honesty always pays double dividends wherever it operates. It is the best domestic and foreign policy to live by.

- The intent of **deception** is selfish gain.
- **Deception** hides all wicked intentions and covers up all that serves its wicked purpose.
- **Deception** is as smooth as a tangled spider's web—when it finishes its weaving it can strangle a lion.
- He who underestimates **deception** becomes its next horrified victim.

Principle	*Comment*

41. Accountable leaders should walk openly in the light of God's truth, having "no part dark" that mars their lives.

- A consciousness of God's constant presence leads to consistent transparency before God and man—a blessed walk indeed!

1 Thessalonians 2:10 (NKJV) You are witnesses, and God also, how devoutly and justly and blamelessly we behaved ourselves among you who believe;

42. Accountable leaders walk in the light to the measure of their enlightenment.

- He who walks in the light of God's presence lives uprightly and applies truth joyfully.

1 John 1:7 (NKJV) But if we walk in the light as He is in the light, we have fellowship with one another, and the blood of Jesus Christ His Son cleanses us from all sin.

Principle	**Comment**
43. Since leaders assume the responsibility and the right to lead, their followers also have the right to know all about their behavior.	• Scrutiny does not hurt honest leaders but helps them walk more circumspectly before God and man—it is the acid test.

Mark 4:22 (NKJV)   "For there is nothing hidden which will not be revealed, nor has anything been kept secret but that it should come to light."

44. A leader who sees his definite need for his brethren walks in the light with them, which does him the most good and safeguards him from disastrous pitfalls.	• Being open and honest with others helps us see our need, which is the first step to meeting that need. Deception blinds us from seeing our needs on a daily basis.

Hebrews 10:24-25 (NIV)   And let us consider how we may spur one another on toward love and good deeds. {25} Let us not give up meeting together, as some are in the habit of doing, but let us encourage one another—and all the more as you see the Day approaching.

Principle	**Comment**
45. A subtle leader who lacks transparency with his followers will eventually find himself on an island alone, being afflicted by his regrets.	• Subtlety is the worst form of deception. It stems from being twisted inside, though it may appear on the outside that a leader is walking straight.

Psalms 32:2 (NKJV)   Blessed is the man to whom the LORD does not impute iniquity, and in whose spirit there is no deceit.

---

46. A leader who lives in a glass house had better live uprightly before God and man, and not criticize others.	• He who lives right has no need to fear stones. The condition of a leader's heart determines his behavior.

Ezekiel 18:5-9 (NKJV)   "But if a man is just and does what is lawful and right; {6}...{9} if he has walked in My statutes and kept My judgments faithfully; he is just; he shall surely live!" Says the Lord GOD.

	Principle	**Comment**

47. Whatever is hidden inside a leader will eventually surface and reveal his motives and intentions, whether they are of God.

- Hidden foxes will continue to grow bigger and will eventually come out of their den and attack viciously and mercilessly. Subtlety is dangerous.

Acts 5:38-39 (NKJV) *"And now I say to you, keep away from these men and let them alone; for if this plan or this work is of men, it will come to nothing; {39} but if it is of God, you cannot overthrow it; lest you even be found to fight against God."*

---

48. Four things in the life of a leader cannot be hidden—covetousness, poverty, love, and pride.

- Nothing can be hidden forever. It is impossible to deceive all the people all the time.

1 Samuel 18:8-9 (NIV) *Saul was very angry; this refrain galled him. "They have credited David with tens of thousands," he thought, "but me with only thousands. What more can he get but the kingdom?" {9} And from that time on Saul kept a jealous eye on David.*

3. Is gracious

Leaders who appreciate the grace of God become gracious in their attitude toward others. **Graciousness:**

- mellows the spirit and sweetens the disposition
- treats others patiently and kindly
- blesses those who cannot return the favor
- manifests Christ in His fullness in the midst of the contrarinesses of life
- performs in difficult situations without complaining
- breathes contentment where we are and in all that we do
- helps us endure circumstances when we can't enjoy them
- returns kindness for ugliness
- returns sweetness for bitterness
- comforts rather than threatens
- forgives rather than seeks revenge
- pardons due to being rich in mercy

Gracious suspect

An old man was passing through a crossroads where a crime had just been committed. When the police arrived on the scene he was the only one in the area. The police, thinking of him as a suspect, took him to the police station for further investigation. He was thrust into prison pending a court case.

He begged the police to give him his medication on time, being a diabetic. His pleas went unheeded resulting in a medical emergency. He almost died in the emergency room. When he appeared before the judge the next day, he explained what he had observed regarding those who committed the crime. His accurate description resulted in the arrest of the two criminals. He was set free to go home, but before his departure he publicly forgave the police who arrested him and prayed for all that were in the court, thus manifesting a gracious spirit.❏

Gracious and forgiving victim

A gracious leader was noted for his loving patience, his tender compassion, his sweet disposition, and his forgiving spirit. He was greatly loved and much appreciated in the community. One day a terrible trial struck his life. A band of criminals invaded his home while he was at work, bound his wife and four little children, and stole everything they could. Upon leaving, they set the house on fire.

At that moment, two police cars happened to pass by and saw the last criminal running fast and jumping into the waiting, loaded truck. One police car followed the speeding getaway truck, eventually catching them. The other patrolman called for the fire department and rescued the family from the fire, which completely destroyed the house.

At the court, after the judge pronounced his heavy penalty on the thieves, this leader asked permission to speak. These were his words, "I forgive you for your crime for Jesus' sake, who forgave me all my sins." He then asked the judge to lessen the sentence. The judge replied, "Justice must prevail!"❏

Principle	*Comment*
49. An accountable leader is gracious in his dealings and in his cooperation with others.	• His graciousness makes him thoughtful in guarding their feelings and considerate of their convictions.

Acts 16:4 (NKJV) And as they went through the cities, they delivered to them the decrees to keep, which were determined by the apostles and elders at Jerusalem.

4. Is a person of integrity

Integrity in a leader beautifies his character and endears him to his people. He is well thought of and highly regarded.

The uprightness of a leader saves him from unnecessary troubles. The integrity of a leader helps him to imbibe sound moral principles to live and operate by. His whole focus is wholesome due to his honesty and sincerity in his relationships and the way he proceeds. Honesty in dealings pays double dividends in the long run.

Honesty and truthfulness are sincere twins that successfully labor together in every endeavor. A man of integrity is honest with himself, with God, and with others. His dealings are void of shady tricks that tend to deceive for selfish gain.

Honest leaders share the praise and acclamation with the people who worked to accomplish the set goal. A man of integrity has a pure mind, void of self-interest. He has honest motives that guide his life. He enjoys wholesome attitudes toward all with whom he deals. His ways are easy to apply, his methods are proven in daily experience. He has clear directions since he is in vital contact with the Throne of God.

True integrity is not for sale

"My integrity is not for sale," was the reply of a leader to his board members who requested that he lower his standards to make it easier on his subordinates in order to entice them for greater production. When he was threatened to be replaced, he refused to waiver in his decision due to his strong and settled convictions. He declared to his board that honesty was the foundation of every lasting successful work for God. His strong stand brought conviction that caused them to repent and align themselves wholeheartedly with him.❏

Righteousness always prevails.

- A man's principles are the gauge of his qualities. He builds his life and stakes his future on them. They guarantee him nobility of character, which will help him stand strong against the tests of time that will assail him, attempting to force him to lower his standards by compromising his principles.
- A man of principle walks uprightly in the midst of crookedness.
- A man of principle does not dilute truth to soften its impact, for fear of offending someone.
- A man of principle does not surrender to gaining popularity at the loss of his divine standard.
- A man of principle lives with settled conviction based on divine principles that are not debatable.
- A man of principle lives with utter faithfulness to all his promises at the cost of his life.
- A man of principle lives with integrity of heart in the face of all accusations without retaliation. He lets dogs bark until they lose their voice and run out of steam.
- A man of principle refuses all the enticements in exchange for his settled convictions; he cannot be threatened into abandoning them.

Principle	*Comment*
50. An accountable leader is a man of principle due to his honest convictions.	• A man of principle is saved from the pitfall of expediency.

John 1:47 (NKJV)   Jesus saw Nathanael coming toward Him, and said of him, "Behold, an Israelite indeed, in whom is no deceit!"

a. walks in truth

Leaders who fulfill truth in their lives are greatly fortified by its penetrating effect and transforming power.

The power of truthfulness

A godly youth asked his godly mother if he could leave their village and go to the far city to learn how to serve God. His widowed mother gave him what her deceased father bequeathed to her and said to him, "I am too old to see you again. Take this $40,000 (which she sewed in his underclothes) and go. I only ask you to promise me one thing my son—always believe the truth, always live the truth, and always tell the truth; and God will bless you all the days of your life." He promised to be faithful to do so.

On his way, while walking the long journey, he fell into the hands of a band of thieves. Two of them asked him if he had any money on him. He said, "Yes, I have $40,000 my mother gave me to study to serve God." They couldn't believe him. So, they brought him to their leader and told him the story. He ordered him stripped of his clothes and discovered the money.

The leader asked him, "How come you told the truth?" He said to him, "I promised my mother to do so all of my life." The leader said, "You have been an example to all of us." As the Holy Spirit convicted them, they all knelt down and repented and promised to serve God like him.❑

Truth is the greatest liberating power on earth. It brings needed security and steps of assurance along the pathway that leads to excellence in character and performance. It is far better to trust the deeds of men rather than their words.

To be an example serves God's purpose far beyond all endeavors. To be an example makes the greatest impact, in that it is truth being exemplified in a totally surrendered life.

Principle	*Comment*
51. An accountable leader aims at being accurate.	• Accuracy is the badge of a noble leader.

Exodus 40:16 (NKJV)   Thus Moses did; according to all that the LORD had commanded him, so he did.

---

52. Accountable leaders abhor falsehood and dishonesty, which characterize the spirit of this age. They refuse to be molded by it, knowing it has ruinous results.	• Being genuine is the greatest saving factor in life. It keeps leaders safe from being swept by the trend that is driving society to the abyss of destruction.

Psalm 26:1-12 (NIV)   Vindicate me, O Lord, for I have led a blameless life; I have trusted in the LORD without wavering. {2}...{4} I do not sit with deceitful men, nor do I consort with hypocrites; {5} I abhor the assembly of evildoers and refuse to sit with the wicked.{6}...{12} my feet stand on level ground; in the great assembly I will praise the Lord.

Principle	*Comment*
53. Accountable leaders are avowed enemies of dishonesty and unfaithfulness.	• They are without guile, an attribute necessary for leaders who desire to reveal Christ.

Joshua 7:19 (NKJV)   Now Joshua said to Achan, "My son, I beg you, give glory to the LORD God of Israel, and make confession to Him, and tell me now what you have done; do not hide it from me."

---

54. No accountable leader ever stretches the truth.	• Honesty gives birth to wholesome accountability.

Ephesians 4:15,25 (NKJV)   but, speaking the truth in love, may grow up in all things into Him who is the head; Christ; {25} Therefore, putting away lying, "Let each one of you speak truth with his neighbor," for we are members of one another.

Principle	***Comment***

55. An honest and steadfast leader keeps his word, even if it is to his own hurt. Once he makes a promise, he is obliged to fulfill it.

- Keeping one's promises reveals nobility of character. It reveals a faithful spirit that rules his life and helps him to be steadfast.

Psalms 15:1-5 (NIV)   Lord, who may dwell in your sanctuary? Who may live on your holy hill? {2} He whose walk is blameless and who does what is righteous, who speaks the truth from his heart {3}...{4}...who keeps his oath even when it hurts, {5}...He who does these things will never be shaken.

- All worthy accomplishments started with the right decision, at the right time, in the right place, going in the right direction. "Right" according to God.
- Honesty in the right direction is the only "right" according to God.
- Leaders are accountable for what they are supposed to do and for what they neglect to do.

b. fights compromise

Compromisers are basically cowards who cannot take a stand for anything. Their fears multiply every time they face a crisis. To compromise for expediency is to please one's self and others rather than God. Man's greatest downfall was caused by **sin,** which is a selfish act for selfish pleasure. Loving God is proved by taking a strong stand in the face of all contrariness of life regardless of the price one has to pay. Compromisers are always losers.

He who has his roots deep in God will dare to take a strong stand for God, His standard, His principles, and His will and purpose on earth. Any leader who makes concessions due to weakening one of his principles for whatever reason, reveals his lack of nobility of character and lack of ability to lead righteously.

When the foundation crumbles...

A leader who once enjoyed a measure of success began to regard having a big name and worldwide fame more important than continuing to uphold the high ethical standard that won him the acclaim of many.

Little by little, he began to succumb to wayward pressures for the sake of gaining wider popularity among popular people. He woke up suddenly to find himself "One of the Big Boys." It excited him greatly as he was in great demand.

Gradually, it dawned on him that he lost self-respect as well as the respect of his early admirers who once regarded him as a model of steadfastness. He became utterly discouraged and oppressed for a season. He confided in his wise wife regarding the devastating feelings of his present condition. She said kindly, sympathetically, yet forthrightly, "When the foundation crumbles, the superstructure is in grave danger." Now he is able to hear and heed her advice. It is far better to be a man of sound principles and be alone, than to compromise and be among the majority whose popularity is a facade.❏

He who learns from the mistakes of yesterday will have a joyful day and brighter future to look forward to. He who wins the battle against compromise will win many battles on different fronts.

Principle	*Comment*
56. Accountable leaders must continually fight their avowed enemy called compromise.	• Compromisers are losers in every battle of life due to their violation of divine principles.

Joshua 24:15 (NKJV)   "And if it seems evil to you to serve the LORD, choose for yourselves this day whom you will serve, whether the gods which your fathers served that were on the other side of the River, or the gods of the Amorites, in whose land you dwell. But as for me and my house, we will serve the LORD."

---

57. Accountable leaders guard against the strong tide of worldly influences, which tend to demoralize their character and lower their standard.	• Walking close to God galvanizes us from outside influences. We are called to influence the world by being flood lights—not just bug lights!

Ezra 10:11 (NKJV)   "Now therefore, make confession to the LORD God of your fathers, and do His will; separate yourselves from the peoples of the land, and from the pagan wives."

---

5. Encourages growth and accountability

Leaders who develop their people to maturity teach them their privileges, responsibility, and accountability.

- **Privilege** is to be enjoyed with a *grateful heart*.
- **Responsibility** is to be carried out with a *diligent will*.
- **Accountability** is to be welcomed with a *serious mind*.

Leaders who develop their people make them valuable assets and increase their productivity.

Leader leads congregation to maturity

A leader attributed his success to determining quality growth in his congregation after he enjoyed quantity growth in great abundance. He held special classes, besides the regular meetings, on three subjects. He also prepared special manuals for those who desired to grow but were unable to attend. His first subject was **Privilege**, the second was **Responsibility**, and the third was **Accountability**.

He taught them on three levels of understanding and progressively increased the details. He did so repeatedly until he noticed the astounding difference of growth in his people. As a result, his church became like a beehive.❏

While preaching is for sinners to come to the Lord, teaching is for saints to grow up in the Lord. Teaching matures saints and enables them to assume worldwide responsibility to reach, preach, and teach where the millions and billions are long awaiting.

The need to develop God's people to fulfill their calling is very crucial in these last days. The need for the fivefold ministry is greater now than during any other generation for the ingathering of the ripened harvest.

Principle	*Comment*
58. A conscientious leader teaches his followers the seriousness of their accountability to God.	• One of the greatest lessons to learn in life is accountability, which restrains from evil.

Deuteronomy 31:7-9 (NKJV) Then Moses called Joshua and said to him in the sight of all Israel, "Be strong and of good courage, for you must go with this people to the land which the LORD has sworn to their fathers to give them, and you shall cause them to inherit it. {8}..." {9}...

---

59. Accountable leaders evaluate people and their performance with the right motive and attitude.	• Proper attitude coupled with appreciation results in proper evaluation.

1 Thessalonians 1:2-7 (NKJV) We give thanks to God always for you all, making mention of you in our prayers, {3} remembering without ceasing your work of faith, labor of love, and patience of hope in our Lord Jesus Christ in the sight of our God and Father, {4}...{6} And you became followers of us and of the Lord... {7} so that you became examples to all in Macedonia and Achaia who believe.

Principle	*Comment*
60. An observant leader assigns responsibilities to people according to their abilities and makes them accountable to him for their accomplishment.	• Where there is no adequate supervision, there will be no satisfactory accomplishment. Proper supervision is the key to productivity.

Exodus 18:25-26 (NKJV)   And Moses chose able men out of all Israel, and made them heads over the people: rulers of thousands, rulers of hundreds, rulers of fifties, and rulers of tens. {26} So they judged the people at all times; the hard cases they brought to Moses, but they judged every small case themselves.

61. Accountable leaders provide the means for their followers to accomplish what is required of them, for this is a vital part of their accountability.	• The best equipment helps produce proper training and the best performance; otherwise, the struggle to accomplish assignments will be laborious and difficult.

Philippians 4:9 (NKJV)   The things which you learned and received and heard and saw in me, these do, and the God of peace will be with you.

6. Avoids blaming and criticizing

Blaming others for our faults doesn't cancel them. He who criticizes himself makes more progress than he who criticizes others. Only when a leader takes his blame does he make progress as he mends his ways.

It was well said that "No one has the right to do what he pleases, except when he pleases to do right." I like to add to it—"right according to God."

Blaming others for our faults may blacken their names but will not whiten ours. Our faults will not be mended by others; they are responsible for their own. Blaming others is basically being an escapist. Only a criminal escapes from the scene of the crime, not the innocent.

If we take heed to the advice and warning of Christ regarding taking care of the beam in our own eyes, we will never waste precious time criticizing others. The best criticism is to do better but say nothing and let our example make a difference practically.

Leaders who avoid blaming and criticizing make greater progress as they will always have the full cooperation of their people. Opening the mouth is the most serious thing in life it has a great reward when inspired by the Spirit of the Lord, but it has great accountability and judgment when not.

Faultfinding needs no special educational course, no talent, no active brain, no decent character, and no deep meditation. It is the gift of gab, a leaking of hot air. He who speaks more than he sees, hears, and observes has no future, nor will he have followers or friends. Some would rather be critical, even if they are wrong, than be right and keep peace. Biting words are full of the venom of self-righteousness that spews its breath of selfishness, which stinks like a skunk.

Overbearing and critical foreman reaps his due

There was a foreman in a factory whose long tongue lashed mercilessly for the least offense at everyone he disapproved of. He did not know how to correct constructively. He was always raging like a wild lion. His people grew sick and tired of his ugly disposition, nasty ways, and volcanic temperament. They agreed to either throw him out of the factory or unanimously out-shout him the next time he began an episode.

The first time, they shouted so loud he couldn't hear his own voice. The second time, they carried him, threw him out, and locked the doors so that he couldn't get back in. The third time, they all walked out and didn't come back to work for the rest of the week. When negotiations started between them and the management, they refused to come back until he was put out of work completely.❑

He that does not know the value of people and how to treat them will not be valued by the people and will be unfit to supervise them.

Justice suffers most in the world due to the misjudgment of the immature, who are quick to utter judgment without giving consideration to facts. Justice brings fairness, regardless of status, nationality, color or creed. Justice treats all people as equals without preference to position. Justice has no favorites. It is blind to personalities high in society. It is deaf to the enticing bribes that bring quick riches but prove detrimental in the end.

The greatest complaints in life are filed against our misjudgments of people and situations beyond our comprehension. Fairness is the willingness to judge others by the same standard we judge ourselves; according to God's principles.

Principle	*Comment*

62. A wise leader must avoid passing the blame, being critical, applying undue pressure, and giving unfair judgment to his followers if he is to lead them harmoniously.

- Only an escapist who is a coward and afraid to face himself passes the blame on to others. Self-justification is the act of accusing others and ignoring accountability.

Psalms 7:3-5 (NKJV) O LORD my God, if I have done this: if there is iniquity in my hands, {4} if I have repaid evil to him who was at peace with me, or have plundered my enemy without cause, {5} let the enemy pursue me and overtake me; yes, let him trample my life to the earth, and lay my honor in the dust. Selah

---

63. An accountable leader will be quick to judge himself but slow to judge others, for he knows the seriousness and the accountability of opening his mouth to deal with the affairs of others.

- Such a leader will succeed because of his honesty before God and man. Judging others should be the last thing on earth, not the first. Justice is the privilege of all in every realm of life.

Romans 2:1 (NKJV) Therefore you are inexcusable, O man, whoever you are who judge, for in whatever you judge another you condemn yourself; for you who judge practice the same things.

	Principle	**Comment**

64. A leader who carelessly passes false rumors about others may ruin their reputations for life; this crime is often committed by immature leaders who haven't learned the seriousness of giving account for opening their mouths.

• Venting our hatred to create prejudice in others reveals a self-righteous spirit. An immature leader falls prey to prejudices, which embitter his life and spoil his relationships with people who could be innocent before God.

Esther 3:8 (NKJV)   Then Haman said to King Ahasuerus, "There is a certain people scattered and dispersed among the people in all the provinces of your kingdom; their laws are different from all other peoples', and they do not keep the king's laws. Therefore it is not fitting for the king to let them remain."

65. An accountable leader does not waste time grumbling and complaining; instead, he invests his time in mending problematic situations.

• It is only as we solve problems that we make progress. Neglected problems don't solve themselves—they produce more.

Colossians 4:5-6 (NKJV)   Walk in wisdom...redeeming the time. {6} Let your speech always be with grace, seasoned with salt, that you may know how you ought to answer each one.

Characteristics & Signs
C. In relationship to HIMSELF

The leader who is true to himself will make faster progress in fulfilling the call of God upon his life. The first prerequisite of being true is the willingness to perform periodic self-examinations, which requires facing one's self. (1 Corinthians 11:28, 31) The second prerequisite is judging one's self. Both require honesty in their entirety. Self scrutiny proves honesty to one's self and a strong desire to reach the height of excellence, which demands the boldness to mend all that stands in the way of ultimate progress.

Honesty leads to true honor. Leaders who are without guile in their spirit enjoy intellectual honesty, a pure heart, and refined desires that have been sanctified by the operations of the Cross and are void of inner conflict. To live with pure motives, a sweet attitude, and a mature understanding of life with all its complications, requires a leader to be conscientious and to systematically apply self-discipline. It necessitates taking his responsibility very seriously and carrying it through with promptness and precision.

Such leaders are fully alert and are quick to observe what God is doing and move with Him, seeing they are sensitized to the leading of His Spirit. No wonder they are on God's honor list!

It was well said by Alexander Pope, "An honest man is the noblest work of God." True indeed. The badge of honesty hangs on the breast of men of integrity who walk straight from the inside and from the outside.

Honesty can be costly
A leader qualified in his field, whose salary was in very high figures and was enjoying a high position, popularity and fame discovered upon his inspection some discrepancies of his operation. Being honest to himself and true to God, he was daring enough to face the issue objectively with the view of rectifying

the matter with his superiors, only to face immediate dismissal and defamation that wrecked his life and affected his family. Honesty is costly; dishonesty is more costly.

The immaturity of the leaders who occupied the high positions made them quick victims of suspicion. They were quick to judge without a thorough investigation. When they discovered their error, pride would not let them apologize to him, but instead they asked him to recant, and enticed him to be reinstated. He said, "I'd rather suffer for my honesty so I can live at peace with myself." The price of honesty is very high, but it is the only way that leads to honor, nobility, and dignity.❑

Principle	*Comment*
66. An accountable leader is an example of holiness, righteousness, godliness, and joyfulness.	• No one becomes what God intended him to be without the discipline of accountability.

1 Kings 3:4-6 (NKJV) {4}...{6} And Solomon said: "You have shown great mercy to Your servant David my father, because he walked before You in truth, in righteousness, and in uprightness of heart with You...."

- Becoming what God has ordained for His leaders to be is most costly in discipline in every area of life.
- Leaders who learn discipline early in life, succeed early in their career and fulfill their calling with great success.
- The daily discipline of the cross cannot be delayed or paid by installments. It has to be paid instantly at every progressive step.

1. Examines and corrects himself

Only leaders who are fully concerned about themselves take inventory with scrutiny and make progress. Every successful business is built on sound principles—which include taking periodic inventories to discover whether the business is succeeding, and making adjustments in policy, personnel, and functions where necessary.

No student knows accurately whether he is going to make the final grade without minor and major tests in the subjects of his interests. The Bible exhorts us in 1 Corinthians 11:28 to examine ourselves and in v.31, to judge and correct ourselves if needed. Such dual action is not an option but a command that must be obeyed, if we are to make progress toward reaching our goal in life.

There are many causes for failure. Some are due to ignorance, lack of self-discipline, lack of carefulness, lack of taking responsibility seriously, etc. Someone said, "It is no use making mistakes if you are not going to learn from them." Correcting our mistakes, after learning the painful lesson, helps us to guard our footsteps in our walk and service for God.

It is never too late to learn new lessons. There is always room for improvement, regardless of where we have reached in life.

One of the greatest tragedies of our time is aspiring to be a leader without first being led.

Know what you can handle or it could ruin you

A young man, urged on by his mother, accepted a position of leadership left vacant by the sudden death of his father. He, being a novice, became frustrated, not knowing what to do or how to proceed. Unable to give appropriate answers regarding major decisions in the business and mounting pressures from his mother resulted in him having a nervous breakdown. His condition became very serious. He was full of fear of recovering and going back to meet further embarrassment.

His uncle, being a knowledgeable and experienced man, intervened and took over the full responsibility. He saved both the boy and the business. He was God-sent.❏

Being a "Momma's boy" does not qualify you to become a leader capable of performing. Discovering our ignorance is the beginning of our quest for knowledge.

Principle	*Comment*
67. A wise leader is not afraid to face himself systematically and correct what is needed, for he realizes that this is the key to progress in his life and ministry.	• Self-examination and self-judgment lead to definite progress. Leaders who correct themselves save themselves great heart-ache and embarrassment, and they always excel.

Psalms 51:2-3 (NKJV)   Wash me thoroughly from my iniquity, and cleanse me from my sin. {3} For I acknowledge my transgressions, and my sin is always before me.

Principle	*Comment*
68. Every leader has to judge himself on issues that matter most to him, and determine the best course of action, not forgetting his accountability before the Throne of God.	• Issues confront all leaders, who must decide their outcome before God. This is proven to require the height of wisdom and patience. Seeking God for His answers guarantees their success.

2 Chronicles 25:14-16 (NIV)   When Amaziah returned from slaughtering the Edomites, he brought back the gods of the people of Seir. He set them up as his own gods, bowed down to them and burned sacrifices to them. {15} The anger of the LORD burned against Amaziah, and he sent a prophet to him, who said, "Why do you consult this people's gods, which could not save their own people from your hand?" {16} While he was still speaking, the king said to him, "Have we appointed you an adviser to the king? Stop! Why be struck down?" So the prophet stopped but said, "I know that God has determined to destroy you, because you have done this and have not listened to my counsel."

He who rejects God's warnings
will suffer God's judgments.

Principle	*Comment*
69. Leaders of all levels should have periodic checkups to see what their office, title, degrees, ministry, and position are doing to them.	• The size of the head tells the true story. When a leader counts all things but dung he lives to glorify God, and he will always be safe.

2 Corinthians 12:7-9 (NIV)   To keep me from becoming conceited because of these surpassingly great revelations, there was given me a thorn in my flesh...{8}... {9} Therefore I will boast all the more gladly about my weaknesses, so that Christ's power may rest on me.

---

70. It behooves every leader, regardless of his level or rank, to realize that there is a day of reckoning coming when he must give account for the stewardship he was entrusted with.	• Leaders must keep their eye on the judgment seat of Christ while carrying out their responsibilities. Such a wholesome attitude is a great saving factor in life. It keeps one pure inside.

Matthew 25:14-30 (NKJV)   "For the kingdom of heaven is like a man traveling to a far country, who called his own servants and delivered his goods to them. {15}... {19} "After a long time the lord of those servants came and settled accounts with them...."

Principle	**Comment**

71. Blessed is the leader who practices self-criticism, for he shall not suffer as much from the criticism of others.

- He who corrects himself needs no other to correct him. It is more beneficial, most purifying, and less embarrassing.

2 Corinthians 13:5 (NKJV) Examine yourselves as to whether you are in the faith. Test yourselves. Do you not know yourselves, that Jesus Christ is in you?; unless indeed you are disqualified.

72. The wisest leader is the one who learns to correct in himself what he sees wrong in others. What a saving!

- Free education is learning from the failures of others; expensive education is insisting on learning from our own.

Matthew 7:1-5 (NKJV) ...{3} "And why do you look at the speck in your brother's eye, but do not consider the plank in your own eye? {4} Or how can you say to your brother, 'Let me remove the speck from your eye'; and look, a plank is in your own eye? {5} Hypocrite! First remove the plank from your own eye, and then you will see clearly to remove the speck from your brother's eye."

Principle	*Comment*
73. Self-judgment with a sincere and pure heart enables a leader to regain his balance and the respect of his followers.	• Honesty of heart leads to constant self-examination, self-judgment, and self-improvement. It keeps a leader on the path of progress.

Galatians 6:3-4 (NKJV)   For if anyone thinks himself to be something, when he is nothing, he deceives himself. {4} But let each one examine his own work, and then he will have rejoicing in himself alone, and not in another.

- The most successful accountable leader is the one who judges himself harder than he judges others.

- The harder a leader judges himself the greater the progress he makes.

- Accountable leaders request no suspended sentences when necessary judgment is due. They know well that delayed justice is injustice of the worst kind.

- Some leaders judge themselves by their feelings, some by their intellect, some by guessing, and some by copying others, while the wise among them judge themselves by God's standards and principles.

a. desires, motives, intents, and attitudes

Pure motives, wholesome desires, sound intents, and right attitudes are a leader's greatest assets. Such attributes lead to the height of successful accomplishments. We all suffer from mixed desires that mislead us in different directions in life until the operations of the Cross are perfected in us. Then we can truthfully exclaim with David, "One thing I have desired of the Lord, that will I seek." (Psalm 27:4, nkjv)

Everything we do in life has a powerful incentive called "motive," which determines our course and the way we operate. Examining our motives periodically and modifying our intentions is a vital part of successful endeavors. People judge us by our actions, God judges us by our motives—why we do what we do.

The attitude we exhibit in everything we do and say is a determining factor, whether we are accepted or rejected. It conveys our feelings, mood, and convictions. Right attitude is an asset that beautifies our disposition as we express our opinions.

Leader's attitudes need refocusing

A leader had an uncomfortable feeling in his heart regarding the way things were going in his operation. In his dilemma he consulted with an elderly, mature, and stalwart leader. After the consultation was over, he realized the heart of the problem was himself. He was suffering from mixed desires that diverted his interests to things other than the main goal. He also was suffering from hidden, selfish motives that drove him incessantly. His attitudes were out of control, running wild. He hurt many of his people.

He took time off to meet God afresh with fasting and prayer. After his encounter with God he found purity of heart and motives, and a sweet attitude that transformed his life and ministry. It was indeed a great comfort and relief to his people. ❑

Principle	*Comment*
74. Accountable leaders constantly check their motives and intentions in their quest for greatness.	• Some are great in themselves, others are great in God. God promotes leaders who are small in their own sight.

Matthew 6:3-4 (NIV) "But when you give to the needy, do not let your left hand know what your right hand is doing, {4} so that your giving may be in secret. Then your Father, who sees what is done in secret, will reward you."

---

75. One of the most difficult examinations a leader has is to continually check his motives for each decision, thought, and move he makes.	• Motives determine the outcome of every decision a leader makes. Pure motives glorify God, bless man, and produce the most satisfactory results.

Proverbs 24:12 (NKJV) If you say, "Surely we did not know this," Does not He who weighs the hearts consider it? He who keeps you soul, does He not know it? And will He not render to each man according to his deeds?

Principle	*Comment*

76. The leader who keeps his motives, attitudes, and desires in check, and alters his path accordingly, is safe to follow.

- Being in tune with God results in being in tune with one's self. Such an attitude is commendable for all leaders who desire intimacy with God.

Acts 16:7-10 (NKJV)   After they had come to Mysia, they tried to go into Bithynia, but the Spirit did not permit them. {8} So passing by Mysia, they came down to Troas. {9} And a vision appeared to Paul in the night. A man of Macedonia stood and pleaded with him, saying, "Come over to Macedonia and help us." {10} Now after he had seen the vision, immediately we sought to go to Macedonia, concluding that the Lord had called us to preach the gospel to them.

- Leaders who are sensitized to the Holy Spirit obey His biddings and forbiddings, and His steps and His stops.
- Accountable leaders who are sensitized to the Holy Spirit are safe and the safest to follow.
- Accountable leaders who succeed in judging their motives rightly will be able to guard their actions rightly.
- Self-opinionated leaders are bad judges of themselves and of others.

b. goals, direction, and functions

Having right goals, clear directions, and proper functions make a leader most effective in pursuit of excellence.

Goals awaken our sense of responsibility, spur us to dynamic action and set our direction in life. Where there's no goal, there's no aim. Where there's no aim, there's no gain. We must always remember there's a **"Go"** in "goal."

A leader's greatest goal in life should be knowing the fullness of God. Such a quest will keep him on the right track as he pursues God's ultimate goal for his life. Life without a worthy goal is like a ship without a rudder in the midst of a tumultuous ocean tossed about unmercifully, until it disintegrates. Having a goal gives meaning and direction to life. It propels us forward with unprecedented gain that helps us maintain a steady impetus. Leaders who have clear directions will reach their goals safely and on time. Leaders who set their hearts on their goals, not on the recompense, will get there early and gain all the rewards as a bonus.

Set your goals high, then attain them

While seeking the Lord on how we could reach leaders of 237 countries and territories with specialized seminars—which would strengthen them to carry on their awesome responsibilities—God spoke clearly to me to *finish the project of preparing leadership manuals that would reach many leaders worldwide and be most edifying, while still pursuing our main goal of continuing to hold leadership seminars.* So far we have 128 titles in different stages of development. (See Appendix B)

The word of the Lord came to my heart very clearly, **"A goal reached must lead us to higher goals."** Another word came to me later, **"Set your goals high, then attain them."** ❏

Accepting the challenge keeps us stretching for God. What a

super delight to be entrusted by God and to trust God in the process of fulfillment. **To Him be all praise!**

Principle	*Comment*
77. A leader who honestly reexamines his functions, goals, and directions periodically and makes necessary changes and adjustments, excels greatly, for the best.	• No operation will make progress without an honest leader who is fully applying divine principles. Such applications guarantee his success without his being sidetracked.

Acts 10:13-15 (NKJV)   And a voice came to him, "Rise, Peter; kill and eat." {14} But Peter said, "Not so, Lord! For I have never eaten anything common or unclean." {15} And a voice spoke to him again the second time, "What God has cleansed you must not call common."

---

78. A leader's greatest enemy is busyness without a worthy goal.	• An ordered life uses every moment constructively, with guaranteed results.

Mark 6:31 (NKJV)   And He said to them, "Come aside by yourselves to a deserted place and rest a while." For there were many coming and going, and they did not even have time to eat.

Principle	*Comment*
79. A leader ought to periodically ask himself, "Where am I in God's plan and purpose?"	• Living close to God will give a leader wholesome directions that lead to the fulfillment of His goals.

Psalms 119:59 (NKJV)   I thought about my ways, and turned my feet to Your testimonies.

---

80. A wise leader asks himself at the end of the day, "Have I given more time to God or to myself?" It is in wise inventory that we know how to make necessary adjustments.	• Time is given to us by God to fulfill His will and purpose on earth; when it is used selfishly, it fails in its mission. The more we value God, the more we value His precious gift of time to us.

Exodus 18:13-24 (NKJV)   And so it was, on the next day, that Moses sat to judge the people; and the people stood before Moses from morning until evening...

- Leaders who make the best use of time are the wisest and the most successful. They will have much leisure time to relax, rejuvenate, think, meditate, and seek the Lord for future guidance.
- Leaders who are time-wasters are life-wasters. They live in a state of utter destitution.

Principle	***Comment***

81. A conscientious leader will ask himself daily, "Where am I in the race?" and also "Am I progressing?"

- Winning the race demands total dedication, absolute concentration, holy determination, and full acceleration.

Philippians 3:12-14 (NKJV)   Not that I have already attained, or am already perfected; but I press on, that I may lay hold of that for which Christ Jesus has also laid hold of me.{13}...{14} I press toward the goal for the prize of the upward call of God in Christ Jesus.

82. The leader who stops once in a while to make sure that he is on the right track stays on course and will reach his appointed goal in due season.

- Sincerity gives birth to carefulness in account-ability. Calculating the outcome of every action we take helps us proceed carefully and wisely.

2 Corinthians 1:12-2:4 (NIV)   ...our confidence testifies that we have conducted ourselves in the world, and especially in our relations to you, in the holiness and sincerity that are from God...{13} ...I planned to visit you on my way to Macedonia...{23} ...it was in order to spare you that I did not return to Corinth. {24} ... {2:1} So I made up my mind that I would not make another painful visit to you...

c. lifestyle

A leader who adopts the lifestyle of Jesus enjoys walking in holiness, righteousness, and joyfulness. There are as many life-styles in life as there are peoples worldwide. Our lifestyle can be influenced by our upbringing, our culture, our environment, our peers, and by all the choices we make at different intervals in life.

It is natural for children to choose their own heroes and change them from time to time. It is common to hear children say, "I want to be like so-and-so, etc." This is one of the instincts in our nature that predominates our lives. Choosing our lifestyle is a major choice that determines our behavior and the way we conduct our affairs.

Dress designers invent new styles of garments periodically while the manufacturers prepare for the marketplace. They give customers limited choices for the four seasons of the year.

In India, the sari industry never makes two saris alike except for the airlines and the hotels. Indian artists have an exceptionally inventive mind to think of every combination of color and design under heaven. They determine the styles the public buys.

To the Christian, Christ gave an exemplary lifestyle to follow. We are influenced by what captivates our desires and likes. In essence, we become like the God we love and worship. This is our lifestyle—Christlikeness.

Christlike lifestyle turns foe to friend

A Christian merchant moved into a remote savage environment with the objective of reaching people for Christ, using his trade as a means. One of the worst residents set his sights on robbing him and eventually killing him as he usually did. He started following him but for some unknown reason he could not get close to him. There was an unseen barrier protecting him.

Nevertheless, he persisted in following the Christian merchant as he went door to door selling his fabric, watching his behavior and mannerisms as he dealt with people. He was convinced in his heart that this man's lifestyle revealed that he was a special breed.

The more he followed the merchant the more he became afraid of him, although he carried no weapons. The stalker kept wondering to himself, "Why haven't I been able to rob and kill this guy, yet? And why am I beginning to fear him?" Upon examining his inner feelings further, he realized that he was beginning to like him.

He continued to follow, but without his sharp machete. That day, he discovered that he was able to get closer to his onetime prey. To his surprise, the fear that had been building in him left, allowing him to get closer to the intriguing merchant. As he did, he began to hear the gospel of Jesus preached all day.

The next day he offered to carry the "preacher's" heavy goods free of charge, just so he could be with him and hear more about Jesus. At the end of the second day, he asked two questions: 1) "How can I become like you?" and 2) "How can I talk to people about Jesus like you do?"

It was a great joy for the preaching merchant to lead his new friend to the Lord. He was able to train him on the job everyday until he became a strong witness for Christ. This was all due to the merchant's Christlike lifestyle.❏

Principle	*Comment*

83. A wise leader needs to consider his lifestyle from time to time and make the necessary adjustments for the best.

- A vision for progress requires sensible action, which requires costly self-discipline— the secret of great accomplishments.

Lamentations 3:40-41 (NKJV)   Let us search out and examine our ways, and turn back to the LORD; {41} let us lift our hearts and hands to God in heaven.

---

84. Every leader should periodically sincerely examine the patterns of his lifestyle and make the necessary changes that will improve his quality of life, relationships, and ministry.

- Progress must cover all areas of life beginning with one's character, which determines his behavior with people and his performance before God and man. Progress is a necessity, not a choice.

2 Corinthians 5:9 (NKJV)   Therefore we make it our aim, whether present or absent, to be well pleasing to Him.

Principle	*Comment*
85. The leader who checks his appetite and disciplines it avoids an early death.	• Leaders who can discipline their desires can successfully control their appetites.

Proverbs 23:2 (NKJV)   And put a knife to your throat if you are a man given to appetite.

---

86. As leaders mature, they begin to study their own peculiarities, idiosyncrasies, and abnormalities, and they concentrate their efforts on correcting them.	• This is an important key to their progress; otherwise, stress increases until it results in distress and misery, hindering their maturing process and causing stagnation.

Psalms 32:4-5 (NKJV)   For day and night Your hand was heavy upon me; my vitality was turned into the drought of summer. Selah {5} I acknowledged my sin to You, and my iniquity I have not hidden. I said, "I will confess my transgressions to the LORD," and You forgave the iniquity of my sin. Selah

---

It is in coming to know Jesus in greater fullness that accountable leaders come to a place of seeing their areas of need and earnestly seeking His available help to make the necessary progress, leading to the full stature of Christ.

2. Is disciplined

Constant discipline is the key to a leader's progress in everything he endeavors to do. Without discipline, life is at a standstill and boring. Discipline is the key to fulfillment in life.

- The undisciplined fail continually for not planning to succeed and for not being willing to pay the price in discipline.
- People who are obsessed with wishful thinking keep wasting their valuable time with no time left to discipline themselves to bring their wishes and thoughts to fruition.
- True freedom is the willingness and ability to discipline one's self in every area of life when the need arises.
- The main purpose of discipline is noble accomplishment.
- Discipline is applying the will power to act upon settled conviction.
- Consistent discipline is a must in order to attain high goals in life.
- **"Don't let what you cannot do interfere with what you can do."** —John Wooden
- Discipline is the key to development of talents, skills, mind, and body.
- The stern realities of life can only be met by stern discipline that cannot waiver.
- The undisciplined person is a burden to his family, a menace to society, and a great expense to the hard working taxpayer.
- The undisciplined person believes life is a long vacation and everybody owes him a living.
- The faithful pay the price in discipline due to believing in a cash-and-carry philosophy.

Disciplined leader's success allows for effective witnessing

A leader whose motto was "Nothing is impossible to the disciplined" proved himself in supervising and leading 300 companies. In the midst of his busyness he held a weekly banquet for people who were high in their companies and witnessed to them about the Lord and their need for Him. Due to his effectiveness in his awesome responsibilities, his testimony and diligence affected the lives of many toward the Lord. He believed that every moment must count for eternity. He knew the value of people, time, and money and used them wisely with notable success.❏

Principle		Comment
87. Accountable leaders are extraordinarily disciplined and enjoy a life of fulfillment.		• There is great gain for leaders who are super-careful and wise in every move they make.

1 Corinthians 9:27 (NKJV) But I discipline my body and bring it into subjection, lest, when I have preached to others, I myself should become disqualified.

Principle	*Comment*
88. An accountable leader has an orderly mind, a disciplined will, and an obedient heart in his daily walk with God.	• Such a trio brings much blessing to a leader's life. It guarantees his smooth sailing in the tumults of life.

Numbers 32:10-12 (NKJV) *"So the Lord's anger was aroused on that day, and He swore an oath, saying, {11} 'Surely none of the men who came up from Egypt, from twenty years old and above, shall see the land of which I swore to Abraham, Isaac, and Jacob, because they have not wholly followed Me, {12} except Caleb the son of Jephunneh, the Kenizzite, and Joshua the son of Nun, for they have wholly followed the LORD.'"*

---

89. An accountable leader is in full control of his temper.	• Accountability is the height of discipline that brings inner stability.

1 Timothy 3:2-3 (NKJV) *A bishop then must be blameless...{3}...not violent but gentle, not quarrelsome...*

Moses lost his temper, then lost his balance and made the wrong decision in breaking the tablet with the Ten Commandments. Finally he lost his opportunity to enter the promised land.

Principle	*Comment*
90. Because accountable leaders are in full control of themselves, they guard against moments of explosive anger, which subtract from their dignity and drain their precious anointing.	• When we submit to Christ's lordship, we are able to master ourselves. His rule over us harnesses our faculties to function properly. His security keeps our emotions in full control.

2 Timothy 2:24 (NKJV) And a servant of the Lord must not quarrel but be gentle to all, able to teach, patient,

---

| 91. A leader who keeps his spirit quiet and his tongue silent will not have to offer an explanation to anyone or give an account for words he has not uttered. | • Better to be eloquent in silence than in words, unless words offer something better than silence. An uncontrolled tongue has caused the downfall of many leaders. |

Proverbs 17:27-28 (NKJV) He who has knowledge spares his words, and a man of understanding is of a calm spirit. {28} Even a fool is counted wise when he holds his peace; when he shuts his lips, he is considered perceptive.

Principle	*Comment*
92. Leaders who do not bridle their tongues are their own worst enemies. They have only themselves to blame here and an account to give before the Lord there.	• A man of God must speak by the Spirit every time he opens his mouth. Spirit-controlled leaders are poised and well-balanced. They ooze with divine wisdom that edifies.

James 3:2 (NKJV)   ...If anyone does not stumble in word,
he is a perfect man, able also to bridle the whole body.

---

93. Every leader must give account for his silence and for his utterance.	• We are accountable for every moment we live and perform in His divine presence.

Romans 2:1-16 (NIV)   ...{6} God "will give to each
person according to what he has done."...{16} this will
take place on the day when God will judge men's secrets
through Jesus Christ, as my gospel declares.

• Leaders who aim to succeed may fail, but leaders who give their best service to others are bound to succeed.

• A successful leader is one whose followers succeed in serving his purpose.

• The beekeeper who takes good care of his bees will have plenty of honey to harvest; so it is with the leader who takes good care of his people.

3. Is conscientious

Conscientious leaders are greatly trusted and entrusted. They always gain the favor of God and man. They are set at liberty to function to their full capacity.

A conscientious leader is noted for his exactitude and mindfulness in all of his dealings. He lives and labors with a fully awakened conscience. His steadfastness and truthfulness guard him from pitfalls that befall leaders of all levels. His transparency is his safeguard, his openness is his credential. He is free from guile in his spirit as well as on his tongue. He is fully trusted and enjoys wide acceptance by all who know him.

God uses consequences of a cleared conscience

A leader was noted for being an excellent law advisor to people in high places. An unfortunate thing happened that devastated him and forced his superior out of office. In his endeavor to be of help to him, he participated in a scandal with the view to cover up and justify what happened. In the process that ensued, he heard the Gospel and surrendered his life to Christ.

His renewed conscience would not give him rest until he admitted his guilt in violating the constitution which he swore to defend and implement. He requested a fair trial and accepted a fair prison sentence which he deserved. It was while he was in prison that God began to use him to share his testimony and win many souls to Christ. It pays to be conscientious.❏

In James 4:17 (nkjv), it says "To him that knows to do good and does not do it, to him it is sin." A sharpened conscience keeps a leader awake until he does what he knows to be right according to God. Conscience is God's gift to keep us right with Him, when it is well-saturated with truth.

Principle	*Comment*

94. An accountable leader is conscientious about everything entrusted to him.

• A leader who is not conscientious is not serious about his accountability.

1 Kings 8:56 (NKJV) *"Blessed be the LORD, who has given rest to His people Israel, according to all that He promised. There has not failed one word of all His good promise, which He promised through His servant Moses."*

A conscientious leader:
- is particular about every thought, word, and deed.
- walks in the light of God's presence.
- lives and speaks the truth even to his own hurt.
- lives with no part dark in his life.
- is forthright—has no shady dealings.
- lives a transparent life before God and man.
- lives with no regrets.
- lives with no alternatives.
- lives with unprecedented liberty.
- lives free from inner subtlety.
- lives free from bragging to impress people.
- lives to please God first and foremost.
- enjoys a continuous flow of fresh revelations.
- enjoys a life of ecstasy.
- is safe to fellowship with.
- is a joy to relate to.
- is free from guile in his spirit.
- is fully trusted by God and man.

a. takes responsibility seriously

Leaders who take their responsibilities seriously accomplish the most and meet their deadlines on time without a struggle. Assuming responsibility elevates a leader in the eyes of his followers as he fulfills his obligations with diligence and precision.

A frivolous attitude takes responsibility lightly and fails in all its endeavors. Such a destructive attitude makes its victim think life is nothing but a joke and laughs at it carelessly. In the final analysis everyone is judged by his own history. The frivolous person is a suspect in society. He cannot be trusted nor entrusted due to his irresponsible attitude which makes him a risk and a liability. D.L. Moody said, "God sends no one away empty except those who are full of themselves." I like to add to that, "and those who are full of foolishness."

Life thrives on the shoulders of those who take their varied responsibilities seriously be it to their homes, church, office, ministry, or society. Failure to produce responsible people is society's greatest default for which it pays a high price. Producing fools who live by their wishes has proven very costly. Prisons, psychiatric wards, and insane asylums are the proof of such an indictment.

Assuming responsibility leads to greater responsibility

A young man met God at an early stage in his life. While studying the Scriptures he realized that God means what He says, says what He means, and backs up what He says by what He does. Such a revelation made a great impact on his life which made him determined to become serious in everything he thought, said, and did. He was apprehended by a fatherly leader who invested his life, time, talents, and substance in him being assured that his investment was not in vain. This young man was entrusted with the awesome responsibility of a gigantic operation at an early age. He proved to be trustworthy due to his seriousness and diligence in life.❏

Lord give us more young men of such caliber who'll be a great blessing to the Kingdom of God.

Principle	*Comment*
95. An accountable leader takes his responsibilities very seriously and performs them diligently.	• God's blessings are God's testings. Testing proves the caliber of a leader's character and performance.

Deuteronomy 6:17 (NKJV)   "You shall diligently keep the commandments of the LORD your God, His testimonies, and His statutes which He has commanded you."

---

96. Accountable leaders are conscientious in every thought, word, and deed, because they are conscious of God's presence.	• Leaders who endeavor to escape from accountability on earth will pay higher premiums before the Throne of God.

2 Corinthians 10:4-5 (NIV)   The weapons we fight with...have divine power to demolish strongholds. {5} We demolish arguments and every pretention that sets itself up against the knowledge of God, and we take captive every thought to make it obedient to Christ,

---

Principle	*Comment*
97. An accountable leader is most reliable in everything he does.	• He is serious in his walk with God and utterly careful in his performance.

Psalms 1:1-3 (NKJV) Blessed is the man who walks not in the counsel of the ungodly, nor stands in the path of sinners, nor sits in the seat of the scornful; {2} but his delight is in the law of the LORD, and in His law he meditates day and night. {3} He shall be like a tree planted by the rivers of water, that brings forth its fruit in its season, whose leaf also shall not wither; and whatever he does shall prosper.

98. Accountable leaders do not coast along with the crowd; they do not count on others, but they lead the way.	• They walk with God, trust Him to lead them, and victoriously forge their way through life.

Numbers 13:30-31 (NKJV) Then Caleb quieted the people before Moses, and said, "Let us go up at once and take possession, for we are well able to overcome it." {31} But the men who had gone up with him said, "We are not able to go up against the people, for they are stronger than we."

Principle	*Comment*

99. Accountable leaders are relentless in their endeavors.

• Diligence challenges the impossibilities of life and gives it a dynamic impetus.

2 Peter 3:14 (NKJV)   ...be diligent to be found by Him in peace, without spot and blameless;

- To lead is to suffer.
- To lead is to bleed profusely at times.
- To lead is to dare the impossible.
- To lead is to challenge people to follow.

b. is fully responsible for his choices

Leaders make their own choices, live by their choices, and are fully accountable for them. Leaders who live by the choices of others fail to accomplish their goal. Leaders who make right choices according to the revealed will of God reap the best dividends.

No leader can afford to guess when it comes to the matter of making decisions. Since there are no small decisions, then we must consider every decision to be very serious. Each decision a leader makes carries with it an awesome responsibility and a great accountability. No leader can afford to be vague when it comes to making decisions pertaining to his responsibility. Guessing is totally out of the picture. It has grave consequences. Indecision is a bad decision that carries with it a terrible penalty.

Leader reveals secret of his success

A successful leader was asked what was the secret of his success. His answer was loud and emphatic, "I have learned to take ample time to wait on the Lord with a seeking heart and an attentive ear. My decisions are the outcome of the revelation of God's will to my heart. I move boldly with the assurance and witness of the Spirit of the Lord."❏

To err in making decisions has plunged many leaders and their operations into failure from which there was no recovery. There can be no room for doubts or hesitancy when it comes to decision-making. A revelation of God's will always comes with perfect peace of mind and full assurance of His confirmation to proceed confidently.

A plaque on a leader's desk read, "The decisions here are 'Maybe' and that is final." So was Sarah's decision in Genesis 16:1-5. She and Abram got in trouble and Israel is still in trouble, and will be until the Messiah returns to rule and reign. Some people live by chance; leaders must live by wise choices. Some live by luck; leaders must live by sure revelation and clear guidance—otherwise, they will be disqualified from their role.

Failed responsibilities affect lives

I was in a foreign country holding a seminar when I received a dinner invitation from a doctor. While in his home, I observed the dinner table being prepared, and noticed a young lady helping who looked very sad.

When I inquired of the doctor if she was sick, he replied, "No, but her fiancé has just broken off their engagement. He flew to the States to attend his father's funeral and there he met another girl, whom he is marrying. To make matters worse, he sent her an invitation to their wedding."❏

Principle	*Comment*
100. Accountable leaders must be responsible and reliable. They must always be aware of the presence of God.	• Assuming responsibility makes a leader shine, while accountability coupled with diligence makes him shine brighter.

Genesis 39:21-23 (NKJV)   But the LORD was with Joseph and showed him mercy, and He gave him favor in the sight of the keeper of the prison. {22} And the keeper of the prison committed to Joseph's hand all the prisoners who were in the prison; whatever they did there, it was his doing....

Principle	Comment

101. Accountable leaders exercise great carefulness in their behavior and performance.

- None of us who are careful will regret it. Carefulness is the key to wholesome accomplishment.

1 Timothy 4:16 (NIV) Watch your life and doctrine closely. Persevere in them, because if you do, you will save both yourself and your hearers.

---

102. No leader who wants to enjoy the privilege of his role can afford to slack off from assuming responsibility, due to his accountability to God and man.

- Watch and pray is the Biblical injunction. Many pray, but few watch. Alert leaders are quick to observe and swift to attend to all their entrusted assignments.

Matthew 26:41 (NKJV) "Watch and pray, lest you enter into temptation. The spirit indeed is willing, but the flesh is weak."

Lack of a strong relationship with God causes inner instability and always keeps a person changing for the worst.

Principle	*Comment*

103. The responsible leader knows the seriousness of making a decision and being accountable for its results.

- Life is made up of decisions for which we must give an account. Each decision has its consequences.

Philemon 1:18-19 (NKJV) But if he has wronged you or owes anything, put that on my account. {19} I, Paul, am writing with my own hand. I will repay; not to mention to you that you owe me even your own self besides.

---

104. The greatest failure in leadership is to be like a chameleon. It is wise for a leader to listen to his advisors and benefit, but ultimately he must make his own decisions and assume responsibility for them.

- Changeableness reveals instability of character because of a superficial relationship with God. Strong relationship with God ensures inner stability and a steadfast walk in the face of changing circumstances.

Proverbs 24:21 (KJV) My son, fear thou the LORD and the king: and meddle not with them that are given to change:

---

c. uses resources wisely

Without divine wisdom, no leader can hope to reach his goal. Wisdom is the principle that sets the pace to accomplish the impossible through wise use of resources. Leaders who live close to God are enriched by His eternal supply and become more useful.

A leader who endeavors to mature his people will be able to utilize their talents and giftings as they develop to their full potential in God.

A leader who knows the value of time and learns to redeem every moment of it for the purpose for which it was intended will accomplish much in a short time. It takes divine wisdom to make the best use of time.

A leader who is faithful makes the most of all the resources God entrusts to him. He must use the means to reach the end. Some novice leaders become entangled in the means until they become the end; then the inevitable happens.

A leader who knows the preciousness of the opportunities God brings his way turns them to his advantage to accomplish his goal without hesitancy.

A leader who understands the necessity of guarding his relationships with people makes an effort to establish and maintain a healthy mutual respect and clear communication. He knows no limit to his sacrifice in serving them for their own benefit.

Well-rounded leaders are mature in their understanding and their outlook. They proceed with the wisdom that gives them direction and answers to solve the problems that arise along the way.

Wise management resurrects failing business

A seasoned leader was called to rescue a failing operation at great sacrifice on his part. He was the only answer on the horizon. He had to arrange the management of his operation at hand which proved a great blessing to many. When he took over the reins he began to seek direction from the Lord with an earnest spirit and a humble heart. God honored him with favor.

He revamped the whole operation, established principles of operation, made his vision and expectations of his people clear, and instilled in them the principles of leadership by giving himself to them and the whole operation. He knew how to mobilize people, how to train them, and how to utilize all their available resources. In a short time the operation began to flourish and God was glorified.❑

Principle	*Comment*
105. No leader who squanders time, words, money, or energy can accomplish anything worthwhile for the Kingdom of God.	• Squandering reveals a lack of gratitude and appreciation of God, and a lack of discipline and wisdom. It indicates insecurity and a lack of contentment.

Proverbs 12:24,27 (NKJV)   The hand of the diligent will rule, but the lazy man will be put to forced labor. {27} The lazy man does not roast what he took in hunting, but diligence is man's precious possession.

Principle	**Comment**
106. The leader who lives under debt will continually fret. He will soon run into his creditors and forced accountability.	• Debt is a result of rebellion against God's laws or a lack of wisdom in managing one's financial affairs.

Proverbs 22:7 (NKJV) ...the borrower is servant to the lender.

---

107. Accountable leaders are careful in their behavior and performance, making them safe to follow.	• We can never be too careful. The more wisdom and discipline we have the more we exercise carefulness.

1 Samuel 2:12-18 (NIV) Eli's sons were wicked men; they had no regard for the LORD. {13}...{17} ...they were treating the LORD's offering with contempt. {18} But Samuel was ministering before the LORD—a boy wearing a linen ephod.

Principle	*Comment*
108. A wise leader knows that a legitimate goal doesn't justify illegitimate practices, and he is careful in his procedures, knowing that he is accountable.	• The fulfillment of God's will and purpose must be done with His help, in His way, time, and place, and with the right motive and attitude in order to please Him.

1 Kings 1:5-14 (NKJV) Then Adonijah...exalted himself, saying, "I will be king"; and he prepared for himself chariots and horsemen, and fifty men to run before him. {6}... {7} Then he conferred with Joab...and with Abiathar the priest, and they followed and helped Adonijah. {8} But Zadok the priest, Benaiah,....Nathan the prophet, Shimei, Rei, and the mighty men who belonged to David were not with Adonijah. {9} ....

d. redeems time

Leaders who value a gift by the value of its giver consider time as the essence of life through which to accomplish the assignments of life.

General's apology for being delayed

A general told his army officer who apologized for being delayed for a few moments, "I have been in the habit of calculating the value of the thousandth part of a second."❏

Everything that is assigned to us by God to be accomplished through our obedience requires time. Until we have a revelation of the preciousness of time, we fail to use it with the same intensity and wisdom it deserves.

The difference between being a success or a failure is how we use time. We all are given an equal amount of time every day. Every moment of it is precious and meaningful when we use it for its intended purpose. The dividing line between success and failure is using or abusing time. Selfishness squanders time in trivialities. Time-wasters are criminals that kill the very essence of which life is made.

God allots all the time for us for what He purposes for us to accomplish. Wasting all or any of it means falling short in its fulfillment. Will we be able to say at the end of our lives, **"It is finished!"** like Jesus did? **Mission accomplished**!

To the fool enjoying time in trivialities is not wasted time. As the adage says, "The fool knows the price of everything but the value of nothing." He who knows not the value of something will not treat it right as it deserves. People who have too much time on their hands, but do not spend enough time on their knees, are always in trouble and wonder why—they keep being **wanderers**.

Double the work in half the time

A student at the Elim Bible Institute, in Lima, New York, was working part-time in a factory that manufactured electrical insulators. To his surprise the management called him to the office and asked him if he would consider working for them full-time. After his shock was over, he said, "First, I am a full-time student. Second, your policy dictates you only give students part-time jobs. Did you change your policy?" He was told that in his four hours of part-time work he produced double what full-time workers ever accomplished.❑

It is not how much time you put in at work, but how much work you put in the allotted time. That was a great testimony to the management of a Christian student who is conscientious, diligent, truthful, and faithful.

Principle	*Comment*
109. Accountable leaders are hard working; they redeem the time wisely and accomplish much.	• Disciplined use of time produces the most when it is harnessed and channeled right.

Ephesians 5:15-16 (NKJV)   See then that you walk circumspectly, not as fools but as wise, {16} redeeming the time, because the days are evil.

Principle	**Comment**

110. Accountable leaders avoid the company of wasters, especially time-wasters.

- He who values God greatly also values time greatly and redeems it for its given purpose.

1 Timothy 6:20-21 (NKJV)   O Timothy! Guard what was committed to your trust, avoiding the profane and idle babblings and contradictions of what is falsely called knowledge; {21} by professing it some have strayed concerning the faith. Grace be with you. Amen.

111. An accountable leader knows that procrastination leads to dark alleys, which end in disappointment, frustration, and deception.

- Procrastination is the dangerous thief of precious time. Procrastinators are pretenders who hide behind a facade of hypocrisy.

Proverbs 6:9-11 (NKJV)   How long will you slumber, O sluggard? When will you rise from your sleep? {10} A little sleep, a little slumber, a little folding of the hands to sleep; {11} so shall your poverty come on you like a prowler, and your need like an armed man.

Principle	*Comment*

112. Some leaders use time wisely, while others abuse it for their own entertainment and don't accomplish that for which it was given. What a great loss!

• Time is what makes life. Wasting time means wasting life that cannot be regained. Time is not a commodity but an absolute necessity.

Ecclesiastes 3:1 (NKJV)   To everything there is a season, a time for every purpose under heaven:

---

113. An accountable leader does not entertain negative thoughts, for they waste time and lead to a life of ease and barrenness.

• Accountability demands having a disciplined and orderly mind. Discipline invigorates the mind to function at its best.

Philippians 4:8 (NKJV)   Finally, brethren, whatever things are true, whatever things are noble, whatever things are just, whatever things are pure, whatever things are lovely, whatever things are of good report, if there is any virtue and if there is anything praiseworthy; meditate on these things.

Principle	**Comment**

114. Foolish leaders live in the past, ignore the present, and are fearful of facing the future.

• A fool is one who has a mind that is undeveloped because of its improper use, due to self-deception.

Philippians 3:13-14 (NKJV)   Brethren, I do not count myself to have apprehended; but one thing I do, forgetting those things which are behind and reaching forward to those things which are ahead, {14} I press toward the goal for the prize of the upward call of God in Christ Jesus.

e. guards the quality of his work

Leaders who take their calling seriously are usually particular about their performance. They are thorough to the end.

The dignity of a leader is determined by his diligence and forthrightness to set a high goal for himself and his operation, and then do all he can to achieve it.

With some leaders it is busyness they boast about; with others it is the quality they employ all their powers to produce. A leader who is particular in his planning, accurate in estimating his timing, and careful in his performance will be sought after because of his insight, foresight, diligence, precision, and perseverance in accomplishing great things that astonish others.

Some leaders were born in a hurry, lived in a hurry, died in a hurry, and failed to accomplish anything worthwhile that could have affected their generation. Other leaders live soberly, put their heart into what they are doing, and reach excellence in everything they do. They live by the motto, "If you don't do it right the first time, you have to keep repeating wasted effort until it is done right."

Quality: the secret to good business

A cobbler, who was charging an enormous sum of money for his work with many customers on a long waiting list, was asked, "Why are people willing to pay so much and wait so long for what you offer? What is your secret?" He said in one word, **"QUALITY**, with capital letters." That was the sign on his shop.❏

Principle	*Comment*

115. Accountable leaders guard the quality of their work while in the race for excellence. There is no sloppiness in their life or performance.

• Accuracy and precision characterize the work of accountable leaders. They are noted for being wise and careful in details.

James 3:13 (NKJV) Who is wise and understanding among you? Let him show by good conduct that his works are done in the meekness of wisdom.

---

116. Leaders who desire to perform in a superior manner must follow the directions of the one they are responsible to and accountable to precisely. They take life seriously.

• Accuracy is a saving factor in life. It saves time, energy, and tempers. Much time is wasted by careless repetitious acts, which reveal a lack of seriousness with God.

Numbers 20:7-12 (NKJV) Then the LORD spoke to Moses saying, {8}...Speak to the rock before their eyes, and it will yield its water..." {9}...{11} Then Moses lifted his hand and struck the rock twice with his rod...{12} Then the LORD spoke to Moses and Aaron, "Because you did not believe Me, to hallow Me in the eyes of the children of Israel, therefore you shall not bring this assembly into the land which I have given them."

Principle	*Comment*

117. No accountable leader ever thinks of being sloppy or lazy.

- Diligence and orderliness lead to excellence in performance.

Proverbs 6:6-8 (NKJV) Go to the ant, you sluggard! Consider her ways and be wise, {7} which, having no captain, overseer or ruler, {8} provides her supplies in the summer, and gathers her food in the harvest.

---

118. Potential leaders who will not perform their duties precisely unless they are under strict supervision and systematic scrutiny are not ready to lead. They are not good followers.

- A leader who needs constant supervision is not disciplined enough to walk with God on his own. Awareness of God's constant presence is the key to depth of commitment.

Matthew 25:24-25 (NKJV) "Then he who had received the one talent came and said, 'Lord, I knew you to be a hard man, reaping where you have not sown, and gathering where you have not scattered seed. {25} 'And I was afraid, and went and hid your talent in the ground. Look, there you have what is yours.'"

---

4. Is alert

Alertness saves a leader from the deception of the enemy. It keeps him on his tiptoes as he moves with God at the speed of the Spirit, Who directs his footsteps in the perfect will of God.

Wasted years
A man slept for 25 years. He woke up when someone was singing, "Wasted years, wasted years! How foolish! Have you wandered in darkness and fear? Turn around, turn around. The Master is calling. He's calling you from a life of wasted years."❏

Sleepwalker
I knew a man who worked for my father during the day, who would walk and talk while asleep at night. His father would sleep during the day so at night he could keep his son from drowning in a big public pool near where he usually walked.❏

Some animals and birds sleep with one eye open while the other is half closed. Conscientious leaders who take their accountability to God very seriously live fully awakened to perform diligently. Alert leaders are discerning, perceptive, and move at the bidding of the Holy Spirit at the same speed and direction. They are fully responsible and reliable.

Vow of attentiveness is leader's foundation
A noted leader was participating in a question and answer session at a conference where he was speaking. The first question directed to him was, "What made you what you are?" His reply was instant and clear: "I vowed to God and to myself to be fully attentive to the voice of God, to concentrate on whatever I am doing, to pay full attention to whoever is speaking to me, to be prompt in my obedience to God, to be conscientious at all times, to show utmost respect to people, regardless of rank and file, and to live with a

sense of my accountability to God and man." It took a long time before the applause subsided.❏

He said much in a little time. It cost him much to achieve all that he had, but it paid good dividends.

Principle	*Comment*
119. An accountable leader is fully alert in every undertaking he assumes.	• Alertness causes a full awakening for excellent performance in God's presence.

1 Peter 5:8 (NKJV)   Be sober, be vigilant; because your adversary the devil walks about like a roaring lion, seeking whom he may devour.

---

120. Accountable leaders must see farther ahead than others.	• They operate from a higher plateau in God.

2 Kings 6:13-17 (NKJV)   ...{14} Therefore he sent horses and chariots and a great army there, and they came by night and surrounded the city. {15} ...And [Elisha's] servant said to him, "Alas, my master! What shall we do?" {16} So he answered, "Do not fear, for those who are with us are more than those who are with them." {17} And Elisha prayed, and...behold, the mountain was full of horses and chariots of fire all around Elisha.

Principle	*Comment*
121. Accountable leaders are open to change for the better: to take on new thoughts and discard the old, stale ones that hinder their progress.	• Taking inventory is necessary for progress. It reveals the areas of weakness and propels leaders forward as they imbibe successful and proven ideas.

Matthew 5:20-45 (NIV) ...{43} "You have heard that it was said, 'Love your neighbor and hate your enemy.' {44} But I tell you: Love your enemies and pray for those who persecute you, {45} that you may be sons of your Father in heaven...."

---

122. Accountable leaders despise the thought of retiring and welcome refiring daily.	• Walking with God and serving Him is a lifetime commitment that carries with it total fulfillment.

Psalms 61:8 (NKJV) So I will sing praise to Your name forever, that I may daily perform my vows.

- A leader who sees as God sees lives with rest in his spirit and enjoys complete freedom.
- A leader who lives with sharp discernment enjoys seeing through realms beyond the natural.

Principle	*Comment*
123. Accountable leaders are always on the alert for the unguarded moment, which has caused the downfall of many who once served God.	• Continual alertness safeguards leaders from the onslaughts of Satan. They are continually sensitized to the Holy Spirit.

Ephesians 6:18 (NIV)   And pray in the Spirit on all occasions with all kinds of prayers and requests. With this in mind, be alert and always keep on praying for all the saints.

| 124. Accountable leaders move slowly toward the fast lane and conquer laziness. | • Wisdom tempers an accountable leader and helps him move with balance. |

James 3:17 (NKJV)   But the wisdom that is from above is first pure, then peaceable, gentle, willing to yield, full of mercy and good fruits, without partiality and without hypocrisy.

| 125. Accountable leaders shun anxiety for their own benefit. | • Anxiety drains nerve energy and weakens the constitution. |

Matthew 6:34 (NKJV)   "Therefore do not worry about tomorrow, for tomorrow will worry about its own things. Sufficient for the day is its own trouble."

III. The Development Process

To be prepared is halfway to where a leader is going; to be trained adequately is the other half—that gets him there. Our success in life depends on the measure of our training, and the speed of our progress depends on the measure of our discipline.

We have a proverb in Jerusalem which says, "He who is aiming to reach the heights must stay up late in the nights," not watching TV but studying arduously. Such leaders become resourceful and enriching to others. They have the capacity and ability to contain, retain, and disperse all needed information pertaining to their field of endeavor. They assume their responsibility with diligence, they labor untiringly, they are ready to face the tests that come their way objectively, and pass with flying colors. They are always watchful and careful to rectify their mistakes without delay. They are resilient and waste no time bouncing back should they fail and fall. Adversity helps them stay on top and gain momentum toward reaching their goal.

The goal reached prepares them for higher goals. Adversity does not daunt them, prosperity does not go to their head and blow it up.

Accountable leaders abhor excuses, knowing that they are the cause of halted progress. They regard excuses as the devil's license to lie so he can go undetected. It is a definite sign of laziness which cannot be covered up. Leaders who resort to a lifestyle of excuses paralyze their activities and grind to a halt. Excuses seem to be a clever way of deceiving others, but they are self-defeating and must have no place, especially in the lives of accountable leaders who live focusing their eyes on the Judgment Seat of Christ in whatever they think, say, and do.

Accountability is one of the most serious things in life that everybody faces sooner or later. Some may not be fully aware of its importance and its fearful consequences as others are. No one will be exempted from giving account for all that has been entrusted to him by God and by man.

The recipe for a successful leader

A gifted potential leader who was very intelligent and fully awakened to perform his responsibility with precision saw his need to be trained under a seasoned leader with many years of experience. He submitted himself to an elderly leader who was resourceful because of many years of rich experience. Knowledge becomes experience with a great price in discipline, while going through the trials, tests, and temptations of life that are necessary for the maturing process. He showed a submissive spirit with much appreciation and received a passing grade. His day came to shine as he assumed a greater role. He glittered like a polished diamond.

His zeal never abated. His vision was progressive. His diligence was incomparable. His performance continued to be excellent. All his behavior was balanced by wisdom. His love for his work never waned; his heart was in it. His patience continued to be stretched to cope with the demands of his increasing responsibilities.

He was faithful to keep his promises. He labored with rest in his spirit. With a strong confidence in God who helped him solve every problem that arose, he met and overcame obstacles along his path. He welcomed added responsibilities with joy and accepted them as new challenges, contributing to his well-rounded growth. He persevered in the face of discouragement and excelled beyond his peers in every assignment.

He was stalwart in faith, always venturing in directions others feared to go. His daring faith was bold as a lion and courageous as a warrior in battle. He learned to manage people, time, and money appropriately and wisely, and as a result he was able to climb to the top of the ladder of leadership with great success.❑

A. How to develop into an Accountable Leader

The measure of our development determines the measure of our success in every field. Development is a choice everyone is able to achieve if he is willing to daily pay the price in systematic discipline.

It is possible for a leader to develop his talents, giftings, skills, intelligence, and ministry. The degree to which he develops depends on his vision in life, his diligence, and the speed with which he pursues his goals.

If a leader fails to develop into an accountable leader, he is bound to fail when he is confronted with tests, trials, temptations, difficulties, hardships, misunderstandings, accusations, stumbling blocks, unreasonable expectations and demands, discouragements, misjudgments, etc., along the path of leadership. The temptation to vacillate, to compromise, to lower one's standard, to choose expediencies above principles, to fear the faces of men, and to retreat in the face of adversity are possibilities leaders of all levels will meet.

Developing into an accountable leader builds a strong immunity against everything a leader will meet and requires:

- Living openly in the presence of God.
- Developing the fear of God.
- Laboring with an eye on the Judgment Seat of Christ.
- Guarding his spirit and motives.
- Guarding his attitudes and thoughts.
- Guarding his speaking and hearing.
- Guarding his actions and reactions.
- Guarding his relationships with God and man.
- Keeping the end in view rather than the pleasure of the moment.
- Learning the seriousness of his accountability to God.

1. Perform efficiently

Accountable leaders develop their skills in order to perform efficiently. They are noted for being excellent in whatever they attempt to do for the glory of God. The measure of their discipline in life and performance supersedes that of other leaders.

It was well said that a man's work is a portrait of himself. It reflects his personality and ability in whatever skills he has mastered producing what he is. He who is satisfied with what he is doing before he reaches excellence is a failure. Someone said, "If you can do better than you're presently doing, then you are lazy." Truth only hurts when resisted, it helps when accepted.

We must always continue to aim higher in order to find lasting satisfaction. We must consider good to be the enemy of better, better to be the enemy of the best, and the best to be the enemy of **excellence,** if we hope to reach to the **height of excellence**.

A leader who hopes to perform efficiently must develop his talents, exercise discipline, refine his skills, advance his knowledge, and concentrate on what he is doing.

Efficiency rises to the top

It was very noticeable in a large business office that the mannerisms and output of a young man were superb. His superior began to test his quality and the speed by which he performed in comparison to his equals. He was incomparable in every way. His salary and hours were increased while the salary and hours of the rest were decreased. No mistakes could be found in what he did. He reviewed his work with precision. He was fast due to his skill. He was entrusted with most of the work in the office because he proved himself. He built a reputation at an early stage in his life and was continually promoted until the day came when he was chosen to be the president of the company.❑

He who is content to stay where he is will never reach where he is supposed to be.

Principle	*Comment*
126. The more a leader considers accountability a vital part of his life, the better he performs every undertaking.	• Accountability spurs a leader on to always be diligent with a determination to be a finisher.

1 Corinthians 9:19-23 (NIV) ...{21} To those not having the law I became like one not having the law (though I am not free from God's law but am under Christ's law), so as to win those not having the law. {22} To the weak I became weak, to win the weak. I have become all things to all men so that by all possible means I might save some. {23} I do all this for the sake of the gospel, that I may share in its blessings.

Principle	*Comment*

127. Accountable leaders exhibit great concern for their work, so they perform carefully and skillfully.

- Love begets concern, which in turn begets carefulness, leading to action. Love is the mightiest driving force on earth.

2 Timothy 2:15 (NKJV)   Be diligent to present yourself approved to God, a worker who does not need to be ashamed, rightly dividing the word of truth.

---

128. An accountable leader is thoroughly occupied and performs joyfully.

- "Occupy till I come" was Jesus' command to those who will obey Him.

2 Peter 1:10 (NKJV)   Therefore, brethren, be even more diligent to make your call and election sure, for if you do these things you will never stumble;

---

a. value resources

Leaders who value their resources use them wisely and efficiently to fulfill their purpose. Resources are valuable means and assets by which plans are accomplished without struggle. The richer the resources, the better the results.

Leaders who realize the preciousness of available resources make the best use of them. Leaders with inventive minds and strong determination make better use of everything by all the means they can. That is why they supersede others in their output.

Develop your resources

A leader of a small outfit was asked how he accomplished so much with so little resources. He said, "I develop the skill of my people, assign specific tasks to each one, supervise them and see that everyone clearly understands their assignments, and teach them to make the best use of their time."❏

A leader's best virtue is the use of the virtues of his people at the cost of high praise.

- **Praise** works wonders in human beings, as it makes them sense that their value to others is being acknowledged worthy of recognition and high commendation.

- **Praise** releases dormant qualities in people that would otherwise stay hidden and untapped.

- **Praise** is the secret that ignites initiatives and helps them gain momentum toward completion.

- **Praise** is the high-octane fuel that keeps a man's spirit stirred up as he moves swiftly toward fulfilling his vision.

- **Praise** is the secret of encouragement, which sustains a man's determination to make continual progress in all his endeavors.

Principle	*Comment*

129. Accountable leaders know the value of time, money, and opportunities, and they use them wisely to accomplish their goal.

- Proper evaluation brings the best results. It is an eye opener as to how to proceed in an orderly manner through proper rectification, if need be.

Ephesians 5:15-16 (NIV)   Be very careful, then, how you live—not as unwise but as wise, {16} making the most of every opportunity, because the days are evil.

---

130. How a leader saves time, money, and energy by revising his thoughts and the way he performs reveals where he is on the ladder of maturity.

- Maturity conserves in order to invest more in the Kingdom of God. It is the only key that guarantees pleasurable fulfillment. It pleases God the most.

Luke 14:28-35 (NKJV)   "For which of you, intending to build a tower, does not sit down first and count the cost, whether he has enough to finish it; {29} lest, after he has laid the foundation, and is not able to finish, all who see it begin to mock him...."

Principle	**Comment**
131. Experienced leaders reexamine their priorities periodically and reorganize them according to God's perfect and revealed will.	• When priorities are set in divine order, life becomes more productive. Leaders who live close to God enjoy His updated agenda. They perform by the dictates of the Spirit.

Galatians 6:3-4 (NKJV)   For if anyone thinks himself to be something, when he is nothing, he deceives himself. {4} But let each one examine his own work....

132. Accountable leaders don't waste their time endeavoring to answer the foolish questions, for they well know that not every question deserves an answer. What a saving!	• Sharp discernment is a great saving factor. Leaders of all people need it in order to be saved from deception and to guard and utilize their precious time carefully.

Proverbs 26:4 (NKJV)   Do not answer a fool according to his folly, Lest you also be like him.

b. pursue set goals

Wise leaders do not waste their time beating the air, nor do they perform haphazardly. They set their short-term and long-term goals wisely and proceed intelligently with determination to reach them. They always stay focused and watch out for subtle distractions along their pathway to greatness.

Leaders who do not work according to set goals are wanderers-at-large. Goals set our directions and the pace by which we reach them. A goal determines a leader's walk and guides his talk. He becomes obsessed by it and proceeds to accomplish it. Undaunted like a lion running after his prey, he cannot be deterred.

Leaders with worthy goals never look backward but always forward. Their eyes are not fixed on the obstacles but on the goal, which keeps them soaring high above the difficulties they meet along the way.

Goals: secrets of success

A leader was noted for his numerous great accomplishments in the field of his calling. He was called to lecture to all types and levels of leaders, revealing the standards, principles, and means and ways by which he operated that made him such a great leader. He declared openly that he set forth fifteen things for his life:

1. I set challenging goals unattainable by many.
2. I set my heart to reach them at any price and denounce discouragement.
3. I become obsessed with each goal; that is all I think about.
4. I stay excited every step of the way.
5. I laugh at obstacles I meet in my path.
6. I never waiver when the path becomes difficult. I work hard to master difficulties I meet.
7. When a goal reaches the realm of the impossible, I exercise my faith in God's ability and availability to help me.

8. I keep focused and refuse the temptation to be distracted or detoured.
9. I refuse to entertain defeat.
10. I shout the victory in every move I make.
11. I work with the assurance of my partnership with the Lord.
12. My commitment to my goals is not debatable but final.
13. I take immediate action at every juncture and refuse to procrastinate.
14. I look forward to each new day with great anticipation.
15. I keep my expectations high and maintain consistent discipline.❏

Principle	*Comment*
133. Accountable leaders who know the value of every opportunity, do well as they pursue their ultimate goal in life.	• No accountable leader is found squandering valuable time. Accountability helps leaders to be their best.

Luke 13:31-33 (NIV)   At that time some Pharisees came to Jesus and said to him, "Leave this place and go somewhere else. Herod wants to kill you." {32} He replied, "Go tell that fox, 'I will drive out demons and heal people today and tomorrow, and on the third day I will reach my goal.' {33} In any case, I must keep going today and tomorrow and the next day—for surely no prophet can die outside Jerusalem!"

Principle	***Comment***

134. Accountable leaders do the things that count the most.

- Accountability in a leader's life makes him a good investor.

1 Peter 4:10 (NKJV)   As each one has received a gift, minister it to one another, as good stewards of the manifold grace of God.

---

135. An accountable leader goes after what he wants in life and usually gets it, for he is a man of action.

- A man of vision is a man of action. Progressive vision moves at the speed of the Spirit and accomplishes the most.

Joshua 14:12-14 (NKJV)   "Now therefore, give me this mountain of which the LORD spoke...It may be that the LORD will be with me, and I shall be able to drive them out as the LORD said." {13} And Joshua blessed him, and gave Hebron to Caleb...as an inheritance. {14} Hebron therefore became the inheritance of Caleb...to this day, because he wholly followed the LORD God of Israel.

---

c. pass the tests

Every promotion is preceded by a successful test. Life is comprised of lessons and tests all the way. Failure or success is the choice everyone makes in every step he takes. **Nothing** is permanent.

We choose failure for not planning to succeed. We make our own choices in life, then our choices shape our character and the way we proceed. He who lets the crowds choose for him will end up where he did not plan to go. Where there is a will we always make a way.

Our tests in life follow the decisions we make. If we choose to walk with God, we don't have to spend the last years of our lives regretting the early ones. Diligent students look forward to testing times to prove their continuing effort to excel. Lazy students prefer the contrary. They hate the finals due to the life of ease which they have chosen.

Student #34

When I was in the seventh grade an incident happened with the laziest student in our class, whom we always called #34. That was how many students we had in the class and he was always the last. One day we were given a four-question math test. It was provoking and hard. To the surprise of the teacher and the students, he finished in only a few minutes. After the teacher recovered from the shock, he reviewed the test and, to his astonishment, discovered that all the answers were correct.

Teachers, because of their many years of experience, become acquainted with all the tricks of students. To fool them is to prove our foolishness. It was summertime and we were allowed to wear shorts. The teacher devised a plan to discover the subtle trick of #34. He called him to the front and asked him to retake the test and write the answers on the blackboard so everybody could see how he suddenly became so smart. He stood before the class with a puzzled look on his face, shaking terribly with fear. He failed to answer even one question.

When the teacher asked him, "How could you succeed in the written test and fail miserably at the blackboard?" he said, "I just forgot." He pretended to squeeze his head but nothing came out because there was nothing there. The astonished teacher noticed the student putting his hands in both pockets and pushing his shorts down. The teacher asked him to pull up his shorts only to discover that he had written the answers on his thighs, where he had copied them during the test. Suffice it to say, he was reprimanded sternly and dismissed. He was not cheating the teacher but himself from the golden opportunity to study, excel, and lead a bright future.❏

Principle	*Comment*

136. Potential leaders who are sheltered and protected will never make the grade in the arena of leadership until they are first tried, tested, and proven.

- We don't know what our responses will be until we are openly exposed to God's testings, the Devil's temptation, and the trials and adversities of human relationships.

Psalms 105:16-22 (NIV) ...{17} and he sent a man before them—Joseph, sold as a slave. {18} They bruised his feet with shackles, his neck was put in irons, {19} till what he foretold came to pass, till the word of the LORD proved him true. {20} The king sent and released him...{21} He made him master of his household, ruler over all he possessed, {22} to instruct his princes as he pleased and teach his elders wisdom.

---

137. No one who aspires to a role of leadership should be considered unless he passes intense personal scrutiny with an "A plus."

- Scrutiny is a must in life with no exception for anyone. It helps sort out the men from the boys; those who mean business with God from those who don't.

Acts 6:3-6 (NKJV) "Therefore, brethren, seek out from among you seven men of good reputation, full of the Holy Spirit and wisdom, whom we may appoint over this business; {4}..."

---

2. Make no excuses for your failures

When a leader makes excuses for his failures they are sure to multiply. Excuses are Satan's license to lie. An excuse is a cover-up lie that requires having an excellent memory.

Why are you here?

A king visited one of the prisons in his capitol. His only question to each prisoner was the same, "Why are you here?" All prisoners had their own excuses to justify themselves except one who told the king that he was hungry one day and being out of work he stole someone's purse and was caught. "Sir, I deserve to be here." Upon hearing such a testimony the king shouted loudly, "Let this prisoner free! How can an honest person live with subtle liars?"❏

Self-justification when we are guilty makes us prisoners, while self-judgment sets us free.

It is costly for a leader to be honest and trustworthy; but to be such pays far more than it costs.

Principle	*Comment*
138. The leader who refuses to make excuses for his failures is on his way up the ladder of success.	• Excuses are the Devil's license to lie and the greatest hindrances to the progress of those who create them.

Micah 7:8-9 (NIV)   ...{9} Because I have sinned against him, I will bear the Lord's wrath, until he pleads my case and establishes my right. He will bring me out into the light; I will see his righteousness.

Principle	*Comment*
139. Accountable leaders do not waste their time justifying their failures. They know that no excuse is acceptable before the Judgment Seat of Christ.	• When we stop excusing ourselves we stop accusing others; then we can make remarkable progress. Self-justification impedes spiritual growth and blocks progress.

Psalms 51:4 (NKJV)   Against You, You only, have I sinned, and done this evil in Your sight; that You may be found just when You speak, and blameless when You judge.

---

140. Owing to the pride of their hearts, the most detrimental problem among novice leaders is their waste of time in defending their failure, and their argument to justify themselves, instead of breaking and humbling themselves, to make progress.	• Pride is the overflow of selfishness, which blinds a leader from seeing his own failures. There is blindness due to birth defects and blindness due to accidents; but willful blindness is the worst. It is deception at its worst, resulting in the total loss of life's intended purpose.

*1 Timothy 3:2-6 (NKJV)   A bishop then must be...
{6} not a novice, lest being puffed up with pride he fall
into the same condemnation as the devil.*

Principle	***Comment***
141. At times a leader's self-justification stunts his growth beyond repair.	• Christcenteredness is the antidote for self-justification.

Luke 10:29 (NKJV)   But he, wanting to justify himself, said to Jesus, "And who is my neighbor?"

---

142. The leader who justifies his sins by pointing at the sins of others, commits a double crime.	• Self-justification leads to self-destruction. It results in much regret, greater judgment, and suffering.

Luke 18:9-14 (NKJV)   Also He spoke this parable to some who trusted in themselves that they were righteous, and despised others: {10} "Two men went up to the temple to pray, one a Pharisee and the other a tax collector. {11} The Pharisee stood and prayed thus with himself, 'God, I thank You that I am not like other men; extortioners, unjust, adulterers, or even as this tax collector. {12} I fast twice a week; I give tithes of all that I possess.' {13}... {14} I tell you...everyone who exalts himself will be humbled, and he who humbles himself will be exalted."

Principle	*Comment*
143. The wisest leader is the one who considers his own faults and finds God's answer. No wonder he makes progress by leaps and bounds.	• He who desires to mend his own ways will have the wisdom of God to help restructure his lifestyle, resulting in a wholesome disposition and performance.

1 Chronicles 21:17-27 (NKJV)   And David said to God, "Was it not I who commanded the people to be numbered? I am the one who has sinned and done evil indeed; but these sheep, what have they done? Let Your hand, I pray, O LORD my God, be against me and my father's house, but not against Your people that they should be plagued." ... {26} And David built there an altar to the LORD, and offered burnt offerings and peace offerings, and called on the LORD; and He answered him from heaven by fire on the altar of burnt offering. {27} So the LORD commanded the angel, and he returned his sword to its sheath.

144. A leader who dares to criticize his faulty performance has come a long way and will still go a long way.	• Self-examination leads to self-criticism and culminates in self-judgment, which is a key to progress and results in peace of mind.

Psalms 41:4 (NKJV)   I said, "LORD, be merciful to me; heal my soul, for I have sinned against You."

3. Strengthen areas of weakness

Leaders who concentrate on developing their weak areas will make astounding progress that will endear them to the hearts of their followers.

We all have areas of need in our lives. If the need is not met in an area it manifests weakness, which results in failure. Knowing our needs is one thing, but endeavoring to meet our needs is another.

We discover our areas of need either by revelation, observation, or failure, or by a real friend who is concerned about our needs and faces us with answers. Proverbs 27:6 (kjv) says, "Faithful are the wounds of a friend." In Psalm 141:5 (kjv) it declares "Let the righteous smite me; it shall be a kindness."

It is to our long-term advantage to strengthen our areas of weakness and become strong in order to excel in all of our endeavors.

Leader succumbs to "hidden" weakness

A famous worldwide leader was found in a mode of behavior that was unbecoming. His fall was disastrous due to his high position. Instead of responding to the help offered to him, he adamantly refused, only to repeat the same embarrassing failure. This was due to an imbedded weakness that revealed an unmet need, which became a major problem in his life, causing his downfall, all of which could have been avoided.

In his first failure there was hope for restoration had he responded to the help offered. Finally, his repeated failure wiped him out completely, a total loss to himself and to the Kingdom of God.❏

Weaknesses in a foundation always endanger the super-structure. A flaw in character is clearly revealed in the presence of strong temptations.

Principle	***Comment***
145. Every wise leader must discover, or seek to know, his weak points in order to rectify them and strengthen himself in the process of serving God.	• If we don't close up loopholes we are liable to sink. Having honesty, truthfulness, and broken-ness of spirit before God is a great saving factor in life.

Job 13:23 (NIV)   How many wrongs and sins have I committed? Show me my offense and my sin.

---

146. What a leader does with his weaknesses when he discovers them reveals his quality and determines his future.	• Determine to be strongest where you are weakest and you will be full of joy and accomplish great feats.

Psalms 119:27-30 (NKJV)   ...{28} My soul melts from heaviness; strengthen me according to Your word. {29} Remove from me the way of lying, and grant me Your law graciously. {30} I have chosen the way of truth; Your judgments I have laid before me.

Principle	*Comment*

147. The leader who really desires the best for himself will pay close attention to his areas of weakness and endeavor to strengthen them by all the means available to him.

- He who pays full price in self-discipline will reap the best of everything. Daily progress is within the reach of every leader who is serious with God, who lives to constantly please Him.

Psalms 139:23-24 (NKJV)   Search me, O God, and know my heart; try me, and know my anxieties; {24} and see if there is any wicked way in me, and lead me in the way everlasting.

---

148. Unless a leader guards against every area of weakness of his life, he will soon find himself swimming in the cess-pools of gross sin, leading him to ultimate disaster.

- Watching leads to discerning, which brings immediate action. Hating sin to the measure we love God is a great saving factor. It is the master key to highly commendable and successful behavior.

Psalms 97:10 (NKJV)   You who love the LORD, hate evil!...

Principle	*Comment*
149. When a leader slips from his position of being in command to second place, there is an inherent weakness in his character. The sooner he deals with it the better, before it brings him to a disastrous end.	• Pressures that leaders go through reveal their strengths and weaknesses. It takes the height of maturity to cope with the responsibility of being the top commander. It is time for leaders of all ranks to grow up and excel.

1 Samuel 13:13-14 (NKJV)   And Samuel said to Saul, "You have done foolishly. You have not kept the commandment of the LORD your God, which He commanded you. For now the LORD would have established your kingdom over Israel forever. {14} But now your kingdom shall not continue. The LORD has sought for Himself a man after His own heart..."

---

150. A leader who measures his performance by his areas of strength but neglects to develop his areas of weakness will be defective in his leadership, which is sure to sink his ship to the bottom of the ocean of self-deception.	• Concentrating on improving demands knowing our areas of weakness through failure and rectifying them. Self-examination followed by self-judgment results in self-improvement —a continual process, regardless of our rank.

1 Corinthians 10:12 (NKJV)   Therefore let him who thinks he stands take heed lest he fall.

Principle	*Comment*
151. The leader who does not work on his own problems will never be able to cope with anyone else's. It will not be long until he and his operation collapse. He will be disqualified.	• Unresolved problems create more knotty problems and plunge a leader into crises, which lead to a disastrous end. Alertness coupled with immediate action is a great saving factor.

Matthew 7:1-5 (NKJV) ...{3} "And why do you look at the speck in your brother's eye, but do not consider the plank in your own eye? {4} Or how can you say to your brother, 'Let me remove the speck from your eye'; and look, a plank is in your own eye? {5} Hypocrite! First remove the plank from your own eye, and then you will see clearly to remove the speck from your brother's eye."

PRESSURES

Added responsibilities, deadlines, commands, requirements, sudden changes, confrontations, disappointments, accusations, unreasonable demands, emergencies, harassments, marriage, children, stress, tension, business, all modes of travel, due bills, obligations of all types, etc.

All the above come to us under the title of unbearable pressures to not only reveal areas of need and strengths, but also to mature us in our character. Everything and everybody's life is formed by various degrees and types of pressure.

Let us welcome pressure and grow up as a result of it.

Principle	**Comment**

152. The leader who is disappointed with himself has just been awakened to realize that he is not what he thought he was, nor is he accomplishing the task he thought he could.

- Disappointments in life are due to lack of fulfillment. The worst disappointments come when we fail to meet our own expectations, which we desire to accomplish in our life span.

Luke 15:17-18 (NKJV)   "But when he came to himself, he said, 'How many of my father's hired servants have bread enough and to spare, and I perish with hunger! {18} I will arise and go to my father, and will say to him, "Father, I have sinned against heaven and before you..."'"

---

153. No leader can be helped until he first recognizes his need and sincerely asks for help. Our greatest need is to see our needs as they really are.

- Desperation makes no hesitation to act. Until a needy leader reaches that point, all efforts to help him are futile. Pride blinds the eyes and hardens the heart.

Jeremiah 49:16 (NKJV)   "Your fierceness has deceived you, the pride of your heart, O you who dwell in the clefts of the rock, who hold the height of the hill! Though you make your nest as high as the eagle, I will bring you down from there," says the LORD.

4. Readily repent and mend your ways

True repentance is a definite sign of a contrite spirit that pleases God's heart. It leads to amendments that develop highly commendable qualities that express Christlikeness.

Repentance is the master key back to God for sinners and saints alike. True repentance follows remorse due to grieving the heart of God. He who repents out of a broken heart really means business with God and breaks away from sin that dominated his life. Change of heart results in a change of behavior and a renewed walk with God on His terms. Some spend most of their lives just being sorry over their pathetic condition, but not enough to repent and break away from sinful living. The richness of God's mercy is always available to those who cultivate a broken heart and a contrite spirit on their way to Calvary.

Repentant killer finds grace, new hope, and a new life

An avowed criminal specialized in killing people who were on the hit list—what a horrible way to make a living. He terrorized his community day and night. He was always one step ahead of the law. He that breaks the law for selfish gain will be broken by that same law. The day came when he ran out of steam. Sin carries with it its own punishment. He exhausted his resources buying sleeping pills, stress pills, relief pills, and everything he could get. He was finally caught and imprisoned with a harsh sentence of many years of unbearable suffering.

While in prison he found himself a captive audience in a special service for dangerous prisoners. God answered the prayers of many on his behalf when he saw himself as God saw him. This revelation of his heart caused him to want to kill himself, but all his attempts failed. About then, his despair turned to desperation and without hesitation he gave his life totally to God with such an outcry that it astonished the authorities and his fellow prisoners, affecting their lives as he experienced the flood of the grace of God. After his release he lived with an ardent faith and a fervent spirit that made him a flaming witness for Christ. He became a glittering jewel for God until his last breath. Many turned to Christ due to his dynamic testimony and godly living.❑

Principle	*Comment*
154. Wrongs in the life of a leader can be corrected when acknowledged and repented of with a sorrowful attitude and brokenness.	• Many live in regret when they could humbly repent and have a new beginning in God. Humility leads the way back to God and restores joy.

2 Corinthians 7:10-11 (NKJV)   For godly sorrow produces repentance leading to salvation, not to be regretted; but the sorrow of the world produces death. {11} For observe this very thing, that you sorrowed in a godly manner: What diligence it produced in you, what clearing of yourselves, what indignation, what fear, what vehement desire, what zeal, what vindication! In all things you proved yourselves to be clear in this matter.

Principle	*Comment*
155. A leader is sensitive in the area where he is guilty. It behooves him to bend and mend in order to recover and get back into circulation, if he is to accomplish what God called him to do and not succumb.	• Sin in the heart produces guilt that overloads the conscience, oppresses the mind, dampens the emotions, and quenches the spirit. It renders its victims helpless, fruitless, and prey to Satan, ending in a wrecked life.

John 3:20-21 (NKJV)   "For everyone practicing evil hates the light and does not come to the light, lest his deeds should be exposed. {21} But he who does the truth comes to the light, that his deeds may be clearly seen, that they have been done in God."

RESTORATION

- **Humility** .... *Paves the way* back to God:
  the attitude .... 1 Peter 5:6

- **Repentance** .... *Leads the way* back to God:
  the will .... Revelation 2:5

- **Brokenness** .... *Walks the wa*y back to God:
  the spirit .... Psalms 51:17

- **Contriteness** .. *Sweetens the way* back to God:
  the heart .... Psalms 51:17

- **Godly Sorrow** .. *Assures the way* back to God:
  the soul ....2 Corinthians 7:10

Principle	*Comment*
156. The leader who does not mend where his need is will soon come to an end.	• Mending is a continual process on the road to maturity and it produces a life of fruitfulness.

Ephesians 4:26-5:5 (NIV) ...{31} Get rid of all bitterness...{32}...{5:3} But among you there must not be even a hint of sexual immorality, or of any kind of impurity, or of greed, because these are improper for God's holy people. {4}...{5} For of this you can be sure: No immoral, impure or greedy person—such a man is an idolater—has any inheritance in the kingdom of Christ and of God.

157. The leader who has not set his mind to discover the measure of pride in his heart and deal with it can never make progress.	• The greatest hindrance and the fiercest enemy in life is pride. It has caused the downfall of many who were on their way to the summit.

Proverbs 26:12 (NKJV) Do you see a man wise in his own eyes? There is more hope for a fool than for him.

Principle	*Comment*
158. The leader who keeps short accounts with the Holy Spirit on all matters in question, will make steady progress in his life and leadership.	• Short accounts keep the slate clean and make for continual joyfulness. When we get right with God all things eventually get right with us.

Matthew 6:14-15 (NKJV) *"For if you forgive men their trespasses, your heavenly Father will also forgive you. {15} But if you do not forgive men their trespasses, neither will your Father forgive your trespasses."*

| 159. The leader who accepts the dealings of God will enjoy the leading of God and have clear directions for knowing how to fulfill His will. | • God's dealings and leadings are the means to our perfection. Our full co-operation with Him helps hasten the process and makes it a daily delight. |

Job 2:10 (NKJV) *But he said to her, "You speak as one of the foolish women speaks. Shall we indeed accept good from God, and shall we not accept adversity?"* *In all this Job did not sin with his lips.*

Principle	*Comment*
160. A leader who cannot be reasoned with is a sure misfit.	• No one is fit to be a leader who cannot be reasoned with.

*Exodus 8:19 (NKJV)   Then the magicians said
to Pharaoh, "This is the finger of God." But Pharaoh's
heart grew hard, and he did not heed them,
just as the LORD had said.*

- The harder a leader becomes, the harder he makes it on himself.

- A leader's safety is in his brokenness before God.

- Dogmatism is the "Dead End" that proud leaders suffer from.

5. Learn from adversity and prosperity

Adversity teaches leaders to live close to God and draw upon His grace. **Prosperity** teaches leaders that their safety lies in their humility with a heart that overflows with appreciation, acknowledging God's goodness.

The leader who is swimming against the stream of adversity discovers either the extent of his strength or the measure of his weakness. It is only after we make these discoveries in our lives that we make our new adjustments toward progress.

Adversities prepare us for reaching ultimate greatness in the open arena as the laborious training of an athlete prepares him for open games. Self-discovery is made possible in the midst of the contrarinesses of life. Listen to Paul's advice in 1 Corinthians 10:12 (nkjv), "...let him who thinks he stands take heed lest he fall." Adversities show us we are not what we think we are, nor are we what other people think we are. We are what we manifest under pressure.

A rough diamond is worthless unless it undergoes the arduous task of polishing, which gives it its glittery shine and makes it worthy of admiration and the high price paid for it.

The education that comes through adversity is lasting in its effect. It destroys all hidden pride and superficiality lurking in us. Adversity is a stern teacher that saves us time as it comes directly to the point it intended to teach. It triggers a new process of becoming more serious in our growth as we aim to reach our ultimate in God. There are no audit students in her classroom, all must be tested sorely and pass the tests. They are graded on the spot depending on their immediate response. He who welcomes adversities with great anticipation will learn valuable lessons that make him more mature.

In prosperity we learn that it pays to obey God explicitly, promptly, and consistently. In Deuteronomy 11:26-28, God put the terms for prosperity: a blessing if you obey. Though our obedience is intended to honor God and please Him, it also releases His blessing on us. When God's blessings go to our head, they hurt us as we tend to take God for granted and take advantage of Him. Many were hurt by prosperity, few by adversity. When God's blessings go to our hearts they fill us with praise, worship, and appreciation for His love and grace.

The friends that we make in our adversities supersede the quality of the ones we make in prosperity. They go through with us, not only gaze at us. The friends we make in prosperity must be tried in our adversity to be proven worthy of our continued trust.

False prosperity puts us in debt while true prosperity keeps us above debt because it comes as a result of the blessings of the Lord. That is the difference between genuine prosperity which is affordable, and the superficial which is most destructive and short-lived. Prosperity presents a greater challenge, requiring more wisdom and direction than adversity does. He who slacks in the time of prosperity will soon lose it only to live with regrets. Superficial prosperity tends to destroy **virtue**; it lives with a false license to do its own thing for its own pleasure. Superficial prosperity is built on borrowing and being broke at the same time. It is a state of utter deception from which there is little hope of recovery.

A present day Job

A friend whom I've known for many years grew prosperous in his business as he continued to honor God. We used to enjoy weekly prayer meetings in his home. He was honoring God with his substance, witnessing, loving, and fellowshipping with the saints that knew him. A day came when adversity tested him to the core. He lost millions of dollars and became indebted by millions of dollars.

All these losses failed to destabilize him, however, because he benefited from the example of Job who said in Job 1:21 (nkjv), "The Lord gave, and the Lord has taken away; blessed be the name of the Lord." He began living closer to God and continued to seek after God. He knew in his heart God wanted to reveal Himself to him in a deeper way. Through it all he passed the test of maintaining the attitude of loving God and trusting Him for His purpose. The day of restoration came with far greater blessings than in the past and he became a great blessing in his testimony and ministry.❏

Principle	*Comment*
161. Accountable leaders learn from adversity as well as from prosperity.	• Both adversity and prosperity awaken in us a greater sense of carefulness.

Ecclesiastes 7:14 (NKJV)   In the day of prosperity be joyful, but in the day of adversity consider: surely God has appointed the one as well as the other, so that man can find out nothing that will come after him.

Principle	*Comment*

162. Accountable leaders are promoted to greatness by braving their way through adversity and all the contrariness of life.

- Honesty generates boldness by which an accountable leader forges his way through the difficulties of life.

Philippians 3:8-9 (NKJV) Yet indeed I also count all things loss for the excellence of the knowledge of Christ Jesus my Lord, for whom I have suffered the loss of all things, and count them as rubbish, that I may gain Christ {9} and be found in Him, not having my own righteousness, which is from the law, but that which is through faith in Christ, the righteousness which is from God by faith;

163. An accountable leader is always ready for the storms of life because of his diligence in his preparation before God.

- Our effectiveness depends on the measure of our preparation. The stages of preparation vary from time-to-time, depending on the need.

Ephesians 6:13-18 (NKJV) Therefore take up the whole armor of God, that you may be able to withstand in the evil day, and having done all, to stand. {14}...

Principle	**Comment**
164. The more a prospective leader comes under the pressure of responsibility and accountability, the more his reactions reveal what lies within him.	• No one knows what is in his heart and how he will react until he is brought under mounting pressure by outward circumstances and influences from every area of life.

Genesis 26:6-10 (NKJV) So Isaac dwelt in Gerar. {7} And the men of the place asked about his wife. And he said, "She is my sister"; for he was afraid to say, "She is my wife," because he thought, "lest the men of the place kill me for Rebekah, because she is beautiful to behold" {8}...{9} Then Abimelech called Isaac and said, "Quite obviously she is your wife; so how could you say, 'She is my sister'?" And Isaac said to him, "Because I said, 'Lest I die on account of her.'" {10}...

B. Some hindrances to development

Self-neglect is a sign of deception of false perfection. No one is going to take care of us as we would take care of ourselves. Self postponement is a definite sign of laziness, the mother of many problems. Procrastination results in neglected duties that create complications and lead to problems, culminating in crises that plunge us to destruction.

Self-absorption:
A leader who is preoccupied with himself is wasting his time and energy encircling himself. He may make bigger circles but makes no progress in the developmental process.

Self-admiration:
A leader who is always seeking to be highly commended when undeserving plunges himself into singing a solo of his own praise with no audience to listen.

Self-aggrandizement:
A leader who is too busy making himself great has no time to see his own imperfections displayed that necessitate repentance, which is the key to progress and wholesome development.

Self-centeredness:
The leader who is taking care of number one to fulfill his desires, needs, and interests will have no time for somebody else.

Self-gratification:
The leader who caters only to what fits his whims and satisfies his wants is indeed pleasing only himself.

Self-deception:
Blinds a person from seeing his need for correction and rectification.

Self-evasiveness:
Refuses to examine and scrutinize himself and take the necessary remedial steps.

Self-confidence:
He who is confident in his own power and sufficiency to meet his own needs and acts independently of anyone outside of himself, exhibits self-confidence, which is God's greatest enemy in man.

Self-defensiveness:
He who covers up his faults is committing two already, but he who defends them is committing three. This is one of the destructive tendencies that plague human nature.

Self-reproach:
Making promises without intending to fulfill them creates a confidence crisis, resulting in total rejection. Broken promises culminate in broken lives thrown on the heap of wrecked humanity.

Self-dramatizing:
Displaying self-importance without deserving it is indicative of a lack of sincerity. No one can force his self-importance on others; it's only when we live to sincerely serve the welfare of others that we become important to them. No lasting progress can ever be made in life without sincerity.

Sincerity eliminates superficiality and purges a person from subtlety. The meaning of the word sincerity is "without wax"; it is a term borrowed from sculpture. After a sculpture is finished, the only two ways a buyer would know that the work is done right is to call another sculptor or put it in the sun at noonday. Any wax fillings used to cover defects will soon melt. Otherwise, it is "without wax"—sincere.

Climbing to the top on the steps of wise counsel

A young man whose ambition was to reach the height of his career heard a lecture on how to devastate yourself and jeopardize your future. He listened attentively and realized that he was so **haughty and full of himself** that he was unable to benefit from any input, teaching, correction, or rebuke from others.

After seeking wise counsel, he began to open his heart to God with humility and openness of mind that helped him accept the correction that helped him mature. He realized that every step he drew nearer to God was progress toward becoming more like Christ.

The young man was able to successfully reach the peak of his calling because he listened to wise counsel and heeded the advice.❏

Humility of heart leads to an open mind and a receptive spirit. This allows a leader to benefit as he gleans from the input of others, leading to a gain in his performance. Welcoming the contribution of the mature enriches the lives of the younger generation.

ACCOUNTABILITY is an edifying term. It stirs every sleeping atom in us to yield to God.

1. An unrepentant heart

Sin is our avowed enemy. Hiding God's enemy and ours only multiplies our sufferings. We are naked in the eyes of God who is omniscient. A hardened heart does not grieve over sin, so it does not lead one to repentance.

Sin separates us from God and from each other. Sin is the costliest thing on earth. It cost Christ His very life for becoming sin on our behalf. Loving God more than ourselves helps us break away from sin. Genuine repentance brings God's forgiveness, releases us from all bondage, breaks all bad habits, and liberates the conscience from guilt and the mind from oppression. It releases the joy of the Lord in our hearts.

Repentance gives us a new beginning in God.

A heart too hard to repent

A man got saved and began to witness about the saving grace of God with great results. His father refused to leave his wayward ways and follow Christ. His repeated words, "I am too young for that now, leave me alone until on my deathbed." It was not long till he got deathly sick. At the doctor's advice he was taken home from the hospital. His son pleaded with him to surrender his life to Christ. His fainting voice "I can't, my heart is so hard from putting God on hold for so long." What a pity to play games with one's soul.❑

Unless we grieve over sin, we do not see our need to repent of it. The deception of sin blinds us from sensing the consequences. No wonder the Scriptures declare that the way of the transgressor is hard—on himself and on others. Hardness of heart is an early judgment we incur upon ourselves.

Hardness of heart is a choice that has disastrous consequences.

Unexpected death leaves no time for repentance

I knew a young girl who was brought up in a beautiful Christian home and enjoyed the same privileges that her sister and brothers had. While they chose to go to Bible school and serve the Lord like their parents, she chose the opposite direction.

She was giving the whole family a hard time as she refused their counsel, rejected their love, and rebelled against the Lord. One day as she was leaving her home in a hurry and crossing the street, she was struck by a car and died instantly.❏

Principle	*Comment*
165. A leader who hides his jealousy, hatred, fears, lies, and insecurities, rather than dealing with them, paralyzes his leadership.	• Transparency is the hallmark of honesty and nobility of character. We are the safest when we walk in the light of God's truth and sweet presence.

Proverbs 26:24-27 (NKJV)   He who hates, disguises it with his lips, and lays up deceit within himself; {25} when he speaks kindly, do not believe him, for there are seven abominations in his heart; {26} though his hatred is covered by deceit, his wickedness will be revealed before the assembly. {27} Whoever digs a pit will fall into it, and he who rolls a stone will have it roll back on him.

Principle	*Comment*
166. No leader who continually hides, defends, and denies his sin intends to forsake it.	• "You that love the Lord hate evil." We must hate sin before we will repent of it.

Numbers 32:23 (NKJV)   "But if you do not do so, then take note, you have sinned against the LORD; and be sure your sin will find you out."

| 167. Both sin and repentance are words that mean absolutely nothing to leaders who give way to their own lusts and have become calloused and deceived. | • Deception leads to hardness of heart that culminates in waywardness. Self-deception paves the way to an early grave with misery and regret. |

Romans 1:22-25 (KJV)   Professing themselves to be wise, they became fools...{23}...{24} Wherefore God also gave them up to uncleanness through the lusts of their own hearts, to dishonor their own bodies between themselves: {25} Who changed the truth of God into a lie, and worshipped and served the creature more than the Creator, who is blessed for ever. Amen.

Principle	*Comment*
168. Unless a leader confronts his own embedded pride, admitting that he is in reality a sinner and in need of God's mercy, he will never seek God's grace and forgiveness through Christ, neither will he enjoy life.	• Pride blinds a leader from seeing his need for God. It turns the heart against God and hardens it against His truth that sets forth His divine standard to live by. Pride has humiliated many leaders who have had great potential.

1 Peter 5:6 (NKJV)   Therefore humble yourselves under the mighty hand of God, that He may exalt you in due time,

169. A leader who lives with a guilty conscience due to being convicted by the Holy Spirit ends up increasing his misery.	• Sin not repented of results in a guilty conscience and an oppressed mind, which manifest a miserable disposition and a gnawing feeling.

Jonah 1:1-2:10 (NKJV)   ...{2} "Arise, go to Nineveh, that great city, and cry out against it; for their wickedness has come up before Me." {3} But Jonah arose to flee to Tarshish from the presence of the LORD....

Principle	**Comment**
170. Moral deadness in leaders leads them to a destructive end, wrecking their lives and bringing down their operation in shame.	• Unless leaders adopt high standards for their lives and performance, they will come to a dead-end. Compromisers are always losers-at-large.

Luke 22:48 (NKJV)   But Jesus said to him, "Judas, are you betraying the Son of Man with a kiss?"

---

171. Because of the hardness of their hearts, rebellious leaders lose sight of the seriousness of sin and its consequences, and gross evil becomes trivial to them.	• Pride deceives the heart and begets a rebellious spirit, which is the cause of all sufferings. Pride always climaxes in destruction, unless it is recognized and repented of before it's too late.

Exodus 5:2 (NKJV)   And Pharaoh said, "Who is the LORD, that I should obey His voice to let Israel go? I do not know the LORD, nor will I let Israel go."

2. Refusal to examine and correct yourself

Leaders may suffer from Satan's deception and people's deception, but the most dangerous deception is self-deception. It is the hardest to discern and be delivered from. Correction is the way to perfection. He who corrects himself is the wisest. His progress is the fastest.

Sharp discernment is the greatest saving factor from deception. Every act of sin is basically an act of deception. Some people wait until they are near death before they consent to go for medical examination. The wiser we become the more we welcome self-scrutiny as well as the scrutiny of others who care so much about our progress. Some people live in constant fear of dying. They go to the doctor or drugstore for the least cold, cough or minor thing. Everyone is entitled to his own conviction in life.

Health in its entirety, spirit, soul, and body, depends much on the individual becoming his own preventive doctor. As the old adage declares, "An ounce of prevention is better than a pound of cure." Refusal of a person to assume full responsibility for himself is called self-negligence, which is a crime he commits against himself. The Scriptures exhort us to have a renewed mind continually (Romans 12:2) and to also glorify God in our body and spirit. (1 Corinthians 6:19-20)

We cannot divorce ourselves from assuming personal responsibility and expect to make progress. No one can be pushed up a ladder; he has to climb it himself if he is to reach the top. He who paddles his own boat gets where he is going.

Too proud to ask for or receive help

A leader fell, shattering his testimony and his self-esteem. He was offered free help in a rehabilitation center, but he insisted he was okay and would make it back. But the trend continued until the bad became worse, including continuing violations, debt, and animosity. His condition became unbearable, but he still rejected any help offered him. Finally, he lost his family and his followers, and became a hobo living in the gutter.❑

Personal responsibility is an awesome duty; we owe it to ourselves.

Principle	*Comment*
172. When people are grieved while following a way-ward leader, he should know by their protests, complaints, and opposition that it is time to stop and mend his life.	• It is sad when followers have to awaken leaders to their sins because they fail to heed the conviction of the Holy Spirit, which is our greatest saving factor, if we obey Him.

Joshua 9:3-27 (NKJV)   But when the inhabitants of Gibeon...{4}...worked craftily, and went and pretended to be ambassadors...{5}...{14} Then the men of Israel took some of their provisions; but they did not ask counsel of the LORD. {15} So Joshua made peace with them, and made a covenant with them to let them live...{18}...And all the congregation complained against the rulers....

Principle	*Comment*
173. A leader who has trouble with himself and does not mend his ways will have trouble with everybody else wherever he goes.	• Inner complexities reveal unresolved problems. Problematic leaders are a detriment to themselves and their people; they cause problems instead of solving them.

Genesis 4:13-14 (NKJV)   And Cain said to the LORD, "My punishment is greater than I can bear! {14} Surely You have driven me out this day from the face of the ground; I shall be hidden from Your face; I shall be a fugitive and a vagabond on the earth, and it will happen that anyone who finds me will kill me."

- **PRIDE** exalts itself at the expense of humiliating, downgrading, and embarrassing others.
- The anthem of the proud is, "How great I am. How small you are."
- Two dreadful things plague the proud critic:
    - a) Dirty hands from throwing mud at others
    - b) The collapse of the mud hole, causing him to be buried in its mire
- The diligent dig in the mines and find diamonds; critics dig in people and find faults.

a. not facing yourself

A coward is afraid to face himself due to the pride of his heart. Pride endangers leaders far beyond anything else. It stymies their progress.

Cowardice is the major failure of fools who specialize in deceiving themselves through their high self-esteem. Facing oneself on a daily basis is one of the greatest saving factors in life. Many have been hiding from themselves, unable to look in the mirror to comb their hair. That's why they look so shaggy.

James in 1:23-25 exhorts the saints to look into the Scriptures because they help us see ourselves as God sees us. Truth liberates us from cowardice and gives us the boldness we need to face life with all its obligations. He who can face himself at any given time is courageous indeed and will make strides toward excellence.

Ability to see own wrong saves and strengthens friendship

A man walking in the street was heard talking loudly enough for passersby to hear, but too quietly to be fully understood. One man was bold enough to ask him if he was all right, or if he was in distress and needed some kind of help. He replied that he was facing himself to prove his point in an argument with a friend, but found a conflict between his heart and mind. He finally won over his pride and reconciled with his friend. Their harmony was restored, and their fellowship renewed on better terms.❏

Humility sees its own mistakes and dares to admit them and mend them saving time and tempers. Humility is a lifetime of bowing down before God every step of the way. Humility is like a flower that blossoms through all seasons and spreads its fragrance the farthest, affecting the lives of many. Humility is a cloak that beautifies our character, reflecting the virtues of Christ.

There need never be any competition or congestion on the "Highway to Humility."

Principle	*Comment*
174. The leader who refuses to face himself and keeps running away is sure to have a head-on collision with God at every turn.	• Head-on collisions with God because of hidden rebellion produce human wrecks, causing unnecessary suffering and great disappointment.

Proverbs 13:18 (NKJV) Poverty and shame will come to him who disdains correction, but he who regards a rebuke will be honored.

175. A cowardly leader who is afraid to face himself, facts, and issues, is unfit for his position.	• Man's pride blinds him from seeing himself as he really is. Deliverance begins when we dare to face ourselves.

James 1:23-24 (NKJV) For if anyone is a hearer of the word and not a doer, he is like a man observing his natural face in a mirror; {24} for he observes himself, goes away, and immediately forgets what kind of man he was.

Principle	***Comment***
176. Undisciplined leaders are basically cowards who are afraid to face themselves.	• The first and greatest step for progress is sternly facing oneself with strict discipline.

1 Samuel 13:1-15 (NKJV) ...{11} And Samuel said, "What have you done?" And Saul said, "When I saw that the people were scattered from me, and that you did not come within the days appointed, and that the Philistines gathered together at Michmash, {12} ...I felt compelled, and offered a burnt offering."...

• The leader who does not regard his soul neglects his responsibility toward himself at the loss of his privileges. Leaders who care about their life and future are careful in dealing with themselves and in mending their ways the quickest way possible.

• No leader can afford to divorce himself from assuming personal responsibility.

b. not dealing with little weaknesses

The subtlety of glossing over little things has deceived some leaders until it became dangerously threatening. It is much easier to deal with little weaknesses before they become big and difficult to deal with.

Each one of us evaluates and weighs things in life differently. What matters most to one may matter little or nothing to another, depending on the measure of their maturity. Nevertheless, none of us can afford to close our eyes at noon and say that the sun is not shining, nor can we afford to think lightly of the small leak in our boat in the midst of the ocean.

Life demands that we be wise, that wisdom might generate carefulness to be observant, realistic, and take life seriously with all its implications. A little slip of the tongue, a little indulgence in eating, a little sip of alcohol, a little wink to a beauty passing by, a little extravagance in spending beyond one's income, a little negligence of duty can cause a depressing accumulation of issues that turn into problems if they are left unattended. All these and many other "little things" grow to an enormous size and overwhelm us.

Only fools underestimate little things. They are void of the wisdom that sees ahead and focuses on the end results, not just on the thrill at the beginning. This wisdom takes all necessary precautions.

"Just a little leak"

A couple agreed to go out for a short ride to a nearby park. They stopped by a drive-in to buy a couple of hamburgers and french fries. When they parked the car they couldn't sit on the outside bench as it was an unbearably chilly day. They decided to keep the engine running to take advantage of the heater. His wife reminded him that he had neglected to take care of the little leak in the muffler, which he kept promising to fix but never did. Suffice it to say they both died from the exhaust fumes. It was only a little leak, but....❏

Principle	Comment
177. The leader who does not seriously attend to all weakness in his life will eventually be conquered by it.	• Alert leaders take immediate action to remedy the least wrong they discover in themselves and so find favor with God and man.

1 Corinthians 5:6-8 (NKJV)   Your glorying is not good. Do you not know that a little leaven leavens the whole lump? {7} Therefore purge out the old leaven, that you may be new lump, since you truly are unleavened...

---

178. The subtle things in a leader's life that eventually betray him are the little things he ignores; a little habit, a little expense, a little time squandered here and there. Many a ship has sunk because of small, unattended leaks.	• Pet things are dangerous and deceptive by nature. They are to be feared as they develop gradually and unnoticeably into a greater menace. Little things can be more dangerous than big things.

Song of Songs 2:15 (NKJV)   Catch us the foxes, the little foxes that spoil the vines....

Principle	*Comment*
179. Hypercritical leaders are the most nervous creatures in the world. They fear being discovered and confronted.	• Fear paralyzes one's faculties and keeps him from functioning properly, ending up totally useless and discouraged.

Matthew 23:27 (NKJV) *"Woe to you, scribes and Pharisees, hypocrites! For you are like whitewashed tombs which indeed appear beautiful outwardly, but inside are full of dead men's bones and all uncleanness."*

Causes of Hypercriticism

Leaders who do not take heed to the warning written in Romans 12:3 (kjv) "not to think of himself more highly than he ought to," hurt themselves and inflict deep injuries on others.

Some signs of hypercriticism are:
1. Self-righteousness
2. Covering up insecurity
3. Having a false self-image
4. Drawing attention to one's self
5. Inner complexities
6. Constant fearfulness
7. Smartness in wickedness
8. Spewing "skunky" venom
9. Being on the defensive
10. Setting up oneself as a mini-god to be idolized and worshipped

c. defending yourself

It is much better to expose our wrong, confess it, and obtain God's merciful forgiveness than to incur His wrath. Only the proud are blind to their wrong, defending it very strongly, while the humble confesses it with remorse.

He who is good to himself will always mend his ways upon discovery. He who will not be corrected will not be perfected. He who defends his mistakes commits a double offense and makes it hard on himself to correct his error. Defending our wrong is self-defeating.

The greatness of a leader lies in his humility before God and man. True humility begets a Christlike attitude where truthfulness always prevails. A leader is supposed to influence his people and lead them into fulfilling his goal with their full cooperation. Only a weak leader allows the people to influence him thus violating the first principle in leadership. No leader knows his areas of weakness and areas of strength until tests come to reveal them.

The closer a leader lives to God, the stronger his ability will be to lead his people for God. Where a leader is mature, richly experienced, and greatly anointed, people respond to him as they behold his wise and clear direction to lead with full assurance every step of the way.

He defended a wrong to the very end

An old doctor got in an argument with a young doctor and became bitter against him. It was for him to see the wrong on his part, but he kept defending it. That is what pride does to all of us. One day there was a special banquet held for medical doctors with a special speaker addressing important subjects and the latest research.

A friend of the old doctor encouraged him to attend and volunteered to pick him up. He said, "I better not go just in case the young doctor will be there!" Finally he hesitantly consented to go. Job said, "The thing I greatly feared has come upon me." (Job 3:25, nkjv) As soon as they arrived at the parking lot, the other doctor arrived at the same time and parked his car beside them. When the old doctor saw him he raged with a volcanic fit of anger that secreted an abundance of toxins into his system and he fell dead immediately.□

The price of defending ourselves when we are wrong is very costly.

Leaders who obey the great Almighty God become great in His kingdom. Leaders who suffer from an overdose of destructive pride are the greatest losers—like King Saul who suffered the loss of his life and kingdom for the following reasons:

1. He was rebellious in his spirit.

2. He was disobedient in his actions.

3. He was stubborn in his will.

4. He was perverse in his ways.

5. He was contentious in his position.

He rejected God's right to rule over his life by rejecting the word of the Lord.

- Excuses are the highway that leads to failure.
- Excuses guarantee perpetual defeat.
- Excuses cause the downfall of lazy leaders.
- Excuses are the language of expert liars.
- Excuses destroy the future of potential leaders.
- Excuses are abhorred by accountable leaders.

Principle	*Comment*
180. Sensitive areas in a leader's life are those where he is wrong and attempts to protect and defend himself, only to make matters worse.	• We discover these areas by being touchy and explosive when confronted with them. Such a condition keeps a leader on the defensive, hinders his progress, and causes stagnation.

Exodus 32:21-26 (NKJV)   And Moses said to Aaron, "What did this people do to you that you have brought so great a sin upon them?" {22} So Aaron said, "Do not let the anger of my lord become hot. You know the people, that they are set on evil. {23} For they said to me, 'Make us gods that shall go before us; as for this Moses, the man who brought us out of the land of Egypt, we do not know what has become of him.' {24} And I said to them, 'Whoever has any gold, let them break it off.' So they gave it to me, and I cast it into the fire, and this calf came out." {25}...

Nothing is more detrimental to a people than weak leadership—one that is influenced by the people instead of the people being influenced by it.

Principle	**Comment**

181. A leader who continues to create excuses for his failure to produce his best, rather than mending his ways, is in real trouble.

- The time wasted by creating excuses could be redeemed to do our best and save unnecessary heartaches. Excuses are polished lies.

Genesis 3:11-13 (NKJV)   And He said, "Who told you that you were naked? Have you eaten from the tree of which I commanded you that you should not eat?" {12} Then the man said, "The woman whom You gave to be with me, she gave me of the tree, and I ate." {13} And the LORD God said to the woman, "What is this you have done?" The woman said, "The serpent deceived me, and I ate."

182. A stubborn leader who refuses to change himself or his ways is a menace to his followers and cannot be trusted by God or man.

- Stubbornness is the height of wickedness and is a manifestation of cooperation with demonic powers against the will of God.

1 Samuel 15:22-23 (NKJV)   Then Samuel said: "Has the LORD as great delight in burnt offerings and sacrifices, as in obeying the voice of the LORD? Behold, to obey is better than sacrifice, and to heed than the fat of rams. {23} For rebellion is as the sin of witchcraft, and stubbornness is as iniquity and idolatry. Because you have rejected the word of the LORD, He also has rejected you from being king."

3. Disregard for counsel and criticism

Wise leaders seek counsel with a grateful heart and derive great benefit from it. They welcome criticism knowing that it stirs one to come up to his full potential and give his best.

Foolish leaders regard seeking counsel as below their dignity. Proud leaders regard themselves above criticism, while wise leaders see the value, importance, and necessity of both for their advantage and enrichment, and to better qualify themselves to lead more efficiently.

Every bit of advice has a price tag with it. Obtaining a prescription from the doctor is one thing—buying and taking it is another.

Willingness to seek advice must be accompanied by a readiness to pay the price to derive its benefit. The wise man seeks the honest criticism of others for his own progress, while the fool only welcomes the praise of others, even if it keeps him in the rut of his foolishness. Good advice and justified criticism are best heeded when most needed by fools. No wonder they keep increasing in their foolishness to the point of no return.

The more mature a leader is, the more he seeks the counsel of the wise and welcomes and benefits from criticism. Each leader must determine what criticism will do to him. Either it will make him better or bitter, reform him or deform him, advance him or retard him, make him or paralyze him.

Criticism should not crack our confidence and create in us self-doubt; rather, it should help us make sure we are on the right track to better perform with greater excellence.

Each wise leader keeps his self-criticism up-to-date, knowing it is the golden key to his perpetual progress. He also knows that to seek the advice of others is one thing—to take it with full consideration to derive its benefit is another.

What takes top priority in a leader's life determines his course of failure or success.

Leader's hardened heart costs him his position and reputation

A leader who had a likable personality and sweet disposition was going through a crisis that unveiled the hidden rebellion in his heart. Such a revelation can be shocking and can lead us to seek help. It can also harden us and close us up tight, insulating us from any outside help because it is interpreted as an intrusion, infringing upon his privacy.

He chose to disregard any advice freely given to him and vehemently rejected the constructive criticism that could have helped him at the time when it was needed most. He hardened his heart, refused to respond favorably for his own sake, and was dismissed, only to suffer a great loss of position, face, and a promising future.❏

Principle	*Comment*
183. The leader who disregards the counsel of the members of the Body of Christ will find himself like a tent without pegs, doomed to failure and shame.	• The counsel of the wise, heeded when needed, makes us wiser. It is one of the most important essentials in life and a great saving factor. He who listens to the wise becomes wiser.

1 Kings 12:6-16 (NKJV)   Then King Rehoboam consulted the elders who stood before his father Solomon while he still lived, and he said, "How do you advise me to answer these people?" {7}...{8} But he **rejected** *the advice which the elders had given him, and consulted the young men who had grown up with him, who stood before him. {9}...{16} Now when all Israel saw that the king did not listen to them, the people...departed to their tents.*

Principle	**Comment**
184. One cannot place his confidence in any leader who shuns accountability.	• Accountability saves a leader from creating confidence crises, which are the worst in life.

2 Chronicles 32:1-22 (NIV) {1}...{7} "Be strong and courageous. Do not be afraid or discouraged because of the king of Assyria and the vast army with him, for there is a greater power with us than with him. {8} With him is only the arm of flesh, but with us is the LORD our God to help us and to fight our battles." And the people gained confidence from what Hezekiah the king of Judah said. {9}....

185. Some leaders are hypersensitive and cannot take criticism. Others are superficial and cannot take being faced; others are hypercritical and set their standards so high they make life miserable for themselves and everyone else.	• Life is too complicated without God's perspective to direct it. His standard can only be reached by obeying His principles in the power of the Holy Ghost. Leaders who obey out of submission enjoy life the most and produce the best. Their strength will not abate.

Proverbs 19:27 (NKJV)   Cease listening to instruction, my son, and you will stray from the words of knowledge.

Principle	**Comment**
186. A leader who goes un-checked by his superiors and colleagues may become wild and destructive.	• Submission is a willing act that brings one into safety. Without submission we become wild, rebellious, and dangerous.

1 Peter 5:5 (NKJV) Likewise you younger people,
submit yourselves to your elders. Yes, all of you be
submissive to one another, and be clothed with humility,
for "God resists the proud, but gives grace to the humble."

Principle	**Comment**
187. When leaders go un-checked, they may suffer from either extremism, fanaticism, or permissiveness; this causes them to be sidetracked, endangers their relationship with God, hinders their service for Him, and hurts their own people.	• No one is above the law of accountability regardless of his rank. Refusing to submit to higher authority complicates matters, causing everybody and everything to turn against us. Leaders who shun accountability will be dethroned from their position.

1 Kings 14:7-10 (NKJV)   "Go, tell Jeroboam...{8}...you have not been as My servant David, who kept My commandments and who followed Me with all his heart... {9} but you have done more evil than all who were before you, for you have gone and made for yourself other gods and molded images to provoke Me to anger, and have cast Me behind your back; {10} therefore behold! I will bring disaster on the house of Jeroboam,..."

Principle	*Comment*
188. Woe unto the leader who is left unchecked; he will become a menace, a tyrant, and a dangerous dictator that rules rudely.	• Leaders who have no one to hold them accountable travel the road to destruction. No leader can be a law unto himself and ever expect to be safe.

Proverbs 5:11-13 (NKJV) And you mourn at last, when your flesh and your body are consumed, {12} and say: "How I have hated instruction, and my heart despised correction! {13} I have not obeyed the voice of my teachers, nor inclined my ear to those who instructed me!

---

189. No leader who is autocratic and carries a chip on his shoulder can survive a long distance leadership marathon. He is unfit.	• Such leaders are short-lived. People cater to leaders to whom they can easily relate because they have gained their confidence.

2 Chronicles 33:21-24 (NKJV) Amon was twenty-two years old when he became king, and he reigned two years in Jerusalem. {22} But he did evil in the sight of the LORD, as his father Manasseh had done; for Amon sacrificed to all the carved images which his father Manasseh had made, and served them. {23} And he did not humble himself before the LORD, as his father Manasseh had humbled himself; but Amon trespassed more and more. {24} Then his servants conspired against him, and killed him in his own house.

4. Broken promises

Leaders who break their promises create confidence crises, which dissipate cooperation and paralyze their operation. The root problem of broken promises is a lack of faithfulness, which is foundational to developing a healthy character.

- *False* promises reveal .... a *deceitful* personality
- *Empty* promises reveal .... a *hypocritical* personality
- *Doubtful* promises reveal .... an *unstable* personality
- *Forgetful* promises reveal .... an *absentminded* personality
- *Lying* promises reveal .... a *twisted* personality
- *Unfulfilled* promises reveal .... an *unreliable* personality
- *Vague* promises reveal .... a *bewildered* personality
- *Hasty* promises reveal .... an *impulsive* personality
- *Depressive* promises reveal .... a *depressed* personality
- *Faithful* promises reveal .... a *faithful* personality

---

- Faithfulness is a supreme virtue that cements relationships and creates mutual confidence that fortify it.
- Some leaders lose their positions and bright future because of broken promises.
- A leader who keeps his promises consistently reveals his worthiness and the high quality of a disciplined character.
- A leader is no better than his promise and the principles by which he lives.
- The Kingdom of God is built on the shoulders of faithful leaders who can be fully trusted by God and man.
- It is very costly for a leader to keep his promises to God, himself, and his followers, but it is worth any price he pays.

A leader's broken promise revealed

A leader's uncouth behavior was exposed as the Spirit of conviction fell during one of his meetings. Forced to confess, he promised his people that it would never happen again. At his word, they allowed him to remain, but on a probationary basis. But when the Spirit of God fell again, his broken promise was exposed and he was dismissed, devastating the spiritually weak among his people.❏

Compelled confession without remorseful repentance keeps a person too weak to overcome. Only in genuine repentance is sufficient grace released to help us overcome.

Principle	*Comment*
190. Nothing destroys people's confidence in their leaders more than broken promises.	• Broken promises reveal unfaithfulness, disloyalty, and a lack of mutual trust.

Jeremiah 15:18 (NKJV) Why is my pain perpetual and my wound incurable, which refuses to be healed? Will You surely be to me like an unreliable stream, as waters that fail?

Principle	*Comment*
191. A leader who does not follow through with what he promises disqualifies himself as a leader and loses the confidence of his followers.	• Empty promises stem from empty lives that have not been filled with God. Faithfulness guarantees the fulfillment of promises, due to its compelling force.

1 Samuel 3:11-14 (NKJV)   Then the LORD said to Samuel: "Behold, I will do something in Israel at which both ears of everyone who hears it will tingle. {12} In that day I will perform against Eli all that I have spoken concerning his house, from beginning to end. {13} For I have told him that I will judge his house forever for the iniquity which he knows, because his sons made themselves vile, and he did not restrain them. {14} And therefore I have sworn to the house of Eli that the iniquity of Eli's house shall not be atoned for by sacrifice or offering forever."

---

192. The leader who does not make good on his promises creates a confidence crisis, which leads to his downfall.	• Where there is no mutual confidence, there is no mutual cooperation— nothing can be accomplished.

Proverbs 25:19 (NKJV)   Confidence in an unfaithful man in time of trouble is like a bad tooth and a foot out of joint.

Principle	***Comment***
193. The leader who does not keep his promises habitually will soon lose the confidence of his colleagues and his subordinates.	• Dishonesty is dressed up lies that disqualify a leader from his role. The honest back up their promises with their lives. Honesty is the badge of the noble.

Hebrews 10:23 (NKJV)   Let us hold fast the confession of our hope without wavering, for He who promised is faithful.

---

194. A vile leader makes promises but never fulfills them, for he has no intention of doing so.	• Subtlety reveals wickedness of heart. Empty promises reveal inner deception.

Exodus 8:8-15 (NKJV)   Then Pharaoh called for Moses and Aaron, and said, "Entreat the LORD that He may take away the frogs from me and from my people; and I will let the people go, that they may sacrifice to the LORD." {9}...{15} But when Pharaoh saw that there was relief, he hardened his heart and did not heed them....

Principle	**Comment**
195. Nothing degrades a leader in the sight of others more than broken promises.	• He who does not keep his promises will have no one to make promises to. He will suffer from loneliness.

1 Samuel 2:12-24 (NKJV) {12}...{22} Now Eli was very old; and he heard everything his sons did to all Israel, and how they lay with the women...{23} So he said to them, "Why do you do such things? For I hear of your evil dealings from all the people. {24} No, my sons! For it is not a good report that I hear. You make the Lord's people transgress."

5. Insincerity

Sincere leaders shine brighter than flood lights. They enjoy the full cooperation of their people and are able to accomplish more than expected.

- Insincerity reveals a twisted personality that is self-destructive.
- Hypocritical leaders are allergic to truth due to its high price in sincerity.
- Appearing on the outside to be what they are not on the inside has left some leaders empty of the commendable qualities that would make them noble.
- Absence of honesty in a leader makes him a walking question mark.
- Honesty makes a poor leader rich and greatly trusted.
- An insincere leader doubts himself and suffers from a guilty conscience.
- Insincerity strips a leader of a virtue that complements the combinations of necessary virtues in his character.
- The badge of sincerity lies in its transparency.
- Insincere leaders suffer from a guilty look on their face and from doubt in their words.
- Insincerity tortures its carrier like a continuous plague.
- Insincere leaders are short-lived. They are like the lark that rises swiftly to a certain height only to plunge down at a faster speed.

It is pathetic to see some leaders who once enjoyed prestige and honor in high places plunge to dishonor—from palaces to prisons, from respect to loathing—because of the insincerity of their hearts. It was well said, "If you want to know what is in the heart of anyone, give him a high position and watch every step he takes and every move he makes." **Insincerity dishonors its victims after exposing them to the eye of the public.**

Dictator lives in fear

A leader who had ruled his country with cruelty embezzled so much from its rich resources and left his own people to live in poverty. Every time the people revolted, his well-trained army squelched the uprising. He became a multimillionaire at the expense of his people, so he lives in utter fear of being assassinated. He has the cooks eat his food in front of him before he eats it, for fear of being poisoned. He lives in isolation and his health is deteriorating fast. He is a frequent visitor to hospitals abroad because he does not trust his own doctors, either.❏

When we are sincere we live a life of fulfillment. When we are insincere we barely exist and are great losers. **It pays to be sincere at any price.**

Principle	*Comment*
196. Nobody can help an unaccountable leader to do the right thing before God because of his insincerity, inner crook-edness, and hardness of heart.	• The condition of his heart determines the course a leader takes. Out of the heart flow the decisions of life. There are no small decisions; all are important.

1 Kings 13:33 (NKJV)   After this event Jeroboam did not turn from his evil way, but again he made priests from every class of people for the high places; whoever wished, he consecrated him, and he became one of the priests of the high places.

197. The leader who says one thing and means another is dangerous to follow. His guile and twisted person-ality are exposed through his hypocrisy, which betrays him.	• Hypocrisy means being twisted inside while trying to walk straight outside, deceiving people. The hypocrite thinks he can outsmart people by deceiving them, but only deceives himself.

2 Peter 2:3 (NKJV)   By covetousness they will exploit you with deceptive words; for a long time their judgment has not been idle, and their destruction does not slumber.

Principle	**Comment**
198. The leader who seldom thinks of what he has does not count his blessings; the leader who often thinks of what he lacks does not measure his selfishness.	• He who is content has full satisfaction and is free from a complaining attitude. He counts his blessings, not his ambitious wants, due to having crucified desires.

Philippians 4:11 (NKJV)   Not that I speak in regard to need, for I have learned in whatever state I am, to be content:

Contentment is enriching.

IV. The Price

The greater the development of a leader, the more the trials, tests, temptations, and opposition he will encounter along his pathway; not to mention being misunderstood and misjudged.

As a leader forges his way carefully and conscientiously, he will be ridiculed at times, misquoted at other times. All these roadblocks assail him while in quest to reach a high standard of accountability in character and performance.

Integrity speaks quickly and loudly

A leader was offered a large sum of money and a promising role in a company that was known for its shady dealings, if only he would compromise his principles of high integrity. They gave him 24 hours to make his decision, but his reply came at once, an emphatic "No!" It was shocking to all the board members present. He was accused of making a hasty decision without thinking of the advantages offered him. He replied, "All I have seen are the disadvantages of losing my integrity, high standard of sound principles, and a sense of accountability which I cherish dearly."❏

The longer a leader entertains such an enticing offer, the stronger the temptation to yield will be. A leader must execute quick judgment against anything that has a selfish ring.

Regardless of the price a leader has to pay to maintain his integrity, he is a winner-at-large in the arena of public opinion. Life is too short to trifle with and waste it in selfish pursuits that mar a leader's character. The loss of integrity is a leader's greatest tragedy.

A. The price of obtaining accountability

Regardless of the high price a leader has to pay to become accountable, it is worth it all. It promotes him in the eyes of people, it releases greater anointing from God, and it helps him perform his responsibilities with ease and peace of mind.

The price of obtaining accountability necessitates living with divine awareness, love for God more than love for one's self, and living for eternity rather than for the pleasures of time. The dividends far outweigh the price.

Accountability brings liberty to leader

A leader caught the vision of the seriousness of his accountability to God and man. He determined in his heart to reach the place of freedom in spirit that comes by becoming accountable. He began to search the scriptures on the subject and vowed to himself to memorize a scripture a day that had to do with this subject that had set his heart right before God.

After awhile others noticed the liberty he was enjoying in his walk with God. **Richer anointing** was evident upon his life. His ministry flourished, greatly affecting the lives of many.❏

Principle	*Comment*
199. A leader's accountability is the greatest under heaven.	• The greater the role, the greater the responsibility and accountability.

2 Samuel 12:1-25 (NKJV)   Then the LORD sent Nathan to David. And he came to him, and said to him: "There were two men in one city, one rich and the other poor. {2} The rich man had exceedingly many flocks and herds. {3} But the poor man had nothing, except one little ewe lamb which he had bought and nourished;...

{4} And a traveler came to the rich man, who refused to take from his own flock and from his own herd to prepare one for the wayfaring man who had come to him; but he took the poor man's lamb and prepared it for the man who had come to him." {5} So David's anger was greatly aroused against the man,...{7} Then Nathan said to David, "You are the man! Thus says the LORD God of Israel: 'I anointed you king over Israel...{8} I gave you...the house of Israel and Judah. And if that had been too little, I also would have given you much more! {9} Why have you despised the commandment of the LORD, to do evil in His sight?'" ...{10}...{13} So David said to Nathan, "I have sinned against the LORD." And Nathan said to David, "The LORD also has put away your sin; you shall not die."...

1. Opposition increases

There are several *reasons for opposition by people*:
1. They are driven by envy
2. They are driven by jealousy
3. They do not like you
4. They do not love you
5. Clashes of personality
6. They are just being evil
7. They are against everybody, due to inner complexities

Some leaders are crushed by opposition, while others rise to the height of their career because of it—just like the kite that needs contrary winds to cause it to soar in the heavens. The stronger the wind, the higher the kite flies. A mature leader does not feel threatened by opposition; he benefits from it in many ways. It helps him walk circumspectly, administer his affairs wisely, use choice words at the opening of his mouth, and always endeavor to walk in the light before God and man.

Opposition is a form of criticism that applies force to hinder progress. The mature thrives on opposition and rises to new dimensions beyond the norm. Opposition can serve a leader as fertilizer serves the crops to cause them to produce abundantly. Opposition is necessary for leaders. It serves to purify them from any mixture in their lives that gives rise to their opponents.

Opposition awakens complacent leader

A complacent leader who was riding on his laurels found himself slipping away due to having a cold heart. He began to earnestly seek the Lord afresh. God answered his prayers by sending opposition that awoke him to the realization of the seriousness of his awesome responsibility.❏

It is only when we are fully awakened that we function adequately and properly fulfill our destiny. Opposition spurs us to dynamic action and helps us excel where once we fell short of performing with excellence.

Principle	*Comment*
200. Every leader who comes to the forefront has his critics to keep him straight, humble, and pure.	• Anything and anybody that keeps a leader humble safeguards him from many pitfalls. It is worth enduring.

Judges 8:1-3 (NIV)   Now the Ephraimites asked Gideon, "Why have you treated us like this?"...And they criticized him sharply. {2} But he answered them, "What have I accomplished compared to you?"...{3}...At this, their resentment against him subsided.

---

201. The leader with no opposition is in grave danger, for the Bible warns of the dangers for such a leader.	• Opposition awakens in us dormant areas that need to function properly and effectively—it makes us reconsider our ways.

Luke 6:26 (NKJV)   Woe to you when all men speak well of you, for so did their fathers to the false prophets.

---

2. Greater blessings bring greater accountability

As our blessings increase, so will our responsibility to disperse them to fulfill God's intended purpose. God's blessings are God's testings in every realm of life. We must account for whatever God bestows upon us, whether talents, gifts, substance, time, people, position, or relationships. Everything must serve His purpose to fulfill His will and please Him. If we abuse the trust by selfishness we pay heavily for it. There's no greater accountability than that of a leader who has been entrusted with much. Abusing a trust is a crime we commit against God on this side of eternity.

In 1 Corinthians 4:2 (nkjv) the Word declares, "it is required in stewards that one be found faithful." A steward is someone who is handling something that doesn't belong to him. He must give account to the measure of the trust. "To use 'yes' and abuse 'no'" should be a leader's motto. Selfishness always abuses trust, while faithfulness fulfills its required demands and purpose.

Young leader, reminded of his accountability, repents

A young leader whose father enjoyed wide fame due to his integrity of character, anointed ministry, and faithfulness in serving God, was entrusted with a position to administer a large sum of money in relief work. As he continued to prosper due to his administrative skills and giftings, it was noticeable that he began to slip over to the margin. Selfishly mishandling money allowed him to acquire things he never had or enjoyed in his childhood. As the trend continued, he was exposed by the media and brought to shame.

His father intervened by confronting his son with the danger of his inconsistency and warned him of his accountability to God and to the public who trusted him with their substance. He recanted, repented, and vowed to be faithful in every way. Today he is back in the saddle, resuming his speed in the second round. We live to learn, then learn to live.❏

Principle	*Comment*
202. The more God blesses a leader the more accountable he becomes in minute details.	• God's blessings are God's testings; severely so. Blessings must be rightly channeled.

Luke 12:48 (NKJV)   "... For everyone to whom much is given, from him much will be required; and to whom much has been committed, of him they will ask the more."

---

203. Leaders who are seeking God for greater blessings, greater opportunities, and greater usefulness must realize that greater accountability accompanies the responsibility and trust that are given to them.	• The greater the role the more costly the price. Leaders who excel in preparation excel in being and doing their best for God. Great accomplishments are wrought through leaders who are diligent and continually faithful.

Matthew 25:21 (NKJV)   "His lord said to him, 'Well done, good and faithful servant; you were faithful over a few things, I will make you ruler over many things. Enter into the joy of your lord.'"

Principle	*Comment*
204. Leaders are going to give account for what they do with what has been entrusted to them: people, tasks, money, talents, blessings, and opportunities.	• Much is required from those to whom much has been given—especially time, which is desperately needed to accomplish everything. Time is a gift of God that makes up life.

Hebrews 4:13 (NIV)   Nothing in all creation is hidden from God's sight Everything is uncovered and laid bare before the eyes of him to whom we must give account.

---

205. Leaders will give account for all their resolutions and reactions, without an exemption or discount.	• Resolution binds us to promises while our reactions reveal who we really are and the measure of our maturity.

Matthew 12:36-37 (NKJV)   "But I say to you that for every idle word men may speak, they will give account of it in the day of judgment. {37} "For by your words you will be justified, and by your words you will be condemned."

B. The price of not obtaining accountability

Living wildly in the arena of world rebellion—against decency, honesty, and accountability—is most dangerous. It tends to accumulate heavy guilt in the conscience, oppress the mind, and dampen the spirit, causing its victim to live in a state of despair, while in danger of resorting to drugs, alcohol, and all diverse ways to find relief, and finally to end it all. The penalty for not developing accountability brings greater misery than the momentary pleasure of selfish gain.

Unaccountable leaders are lords of their own kingdom, which is built on false premises. They live under condemnation and judgment. Their guilty conscience harasses them continually. They need to consume large quantities of sleeping pills in order to sleep and are nervous wrecks.

Accountability helps a person to be safe, have a healthy self-respect, live with himself, and find it easy to relate to others.

Woe to the leader who has no authority to answer to—not even a committee to monitor his activities and keep him balanced for his safety and the safety of the whole operation.

Authority without accountability leads to rebellion
A high ranking officer plotted against his king, was able to depose him, and took over the reign of his country. He terrorized his people in order to rule them with a rod of iron. He also began to squander money supporting pockets of rebellion worldwide.❏

Where there is no sense of accountability there will be no self-restraint. Such rulers are like wild horses roaming the wilderness, kicking, jumping, racing, and fighting because they are untamed, undisciplined, and untrained. Every leader has his day to revel in fulfilling his dreams without realizing his accountability on Judgment Day. Wild leaders are a menace to society. They are dangerous and will pay a heavy price on the appointed day.

Accountable leaders live with peace of mind, a clear conscience, and a joyful disposition. They enjoy life immensely and revel in the full cooperation of their people.

Leadership is most essential in life...
and in all of life's accomplishments.

- *Absence of leadership* produces chaos.
- *Defective leadership* falls short of accomplishing its goal.
- *Untrained leadership* does not go far in its attempts.
- *Inexperienced leadership* operates with much guessing, resulting in much waste of time, substance, and energy.
- *Copyist leadership* operates with fear of failure and it does.
- *Well-trained leadership* does **good**.
- *Richly experienced leadership* does **better**.
- *Mature leadership* does **best**.

1. Judgment

Leaders who judge themselves will not be judged when they genuinely repent. Judgment punishes when resisted; it purges when accepted. Judgment awakens us to the seriousness of our responsibilities.

Periodic physical checkups are highly recommended in order to know the general state of health and to discover any arising condition that might endanger one's health. So it is spiritually and mentally.

No one can judge himself justly without first searching his heart and submitting his discoveries to God. It is far better to judge ourselves than to wait to be judged. Self-judgment is not an option. It is a "must" that is repeated many times in the Scriptures. Also heeding the all ages advice, "If we would judge ourselves, we should not be judged." 1 Corinthians 11:31 (kjv)

Judge judges himself

A judge was late to an appointment and, like many, he thought he could make up the time by speeding. He was caught and ticketed by the police. When his case came to court he pronounced a double fine on himself and apologized publicly to the police officer who faithfully carried out his duty. He declared openly his violation and said, "I should be an example to the public by my obedience to the law I uphold."❏

Six important virtues are expected of a **judge**:

1. To listen attentively	4. To behave impartially
2. To treat courteously	5. To consider soberly
3. To answer wisely	6. To decide justly

Principle	*Comment*
206. No perverted leader, regardless of his position, fame, or effectiveness in the past, is exempt from judgment unless he exhibits a true spirit of repentance and brokenness before God.	• Repentance is the gateway back to God when evidence of true contriteness is present. True repentance makes us recipients of God's rich mercy, which exempts us from His pending judgment.

Psalms 51:10 (NKJV)   Create in me a clean heart,
O God, and renew a steadfast spirit within me.

The past is past regardless of how bad it has been. Thank God we can have a clean future to look forward to and start all over again if we wholeheartedly repent and meet God afresh. Our God is rich in mercy that exempts us from judgment when we come to Christ.

Life is full of twists and turns, ups and downs, and many times it has some short or long detours. We encounter parallel circumstances in the spiritual realm as we walk with God.

Repentance gives us a new start with God, as well as greater expectations and a brighter future in walking with and serving Him.

Principle	*Comment*

207. Any leader who trespasses the limitations that are resident in the constitution he promised to uphold and violates the principles that apply must be held accountable by the law of justice.

- The most dangerous leaders are those who are a law unto themselves. He who is a god unto himself has his own laws that cater to his whims and desires. Uncrucified desires have caused the downfall of many.

2 Chronicles 26:16-21 (KJV)   But when he was strong, his heart was lifted up to his destruction: for he transgressed against the LORD his God, and went into the temple of the LORD to burn incense upon the altar of incense. {17} And Azariah the priest went in after him... {18} And they withstood Uzziah the king, and said unto him, it appertaineth not unto thee, Uzziah, to burn incense unto the LORD...{19} Then Uzziah was wroth, and had a censer in his hand to burn incense: and while he was wroth with the priests, the leprosy even rose up in his forehead before the priests in the house of the LORD....

Faithfulness coupled with **discipline** keeps leaders in line with their commitments. **Commitment** binds leaders to their promises and enables them to boldly take a strong stand for righteousness.

Principle	*Comment*
208. Leaders lacking in accountability are on society's suspicious list.	• No accountability, no respectability, reliability or acceptance.

1 Corinthians 6:1,7 (NKJV) Dare any of you, having a matter against another, go to law before the unrighteous, and not before the saints? {7} Now therefore, it is already an utter failure for you that you go to law against one another....

---

209. Well-rounded leaders who eat square meals don't stay around long. They pay heavily for exceeding the "feed" limit.	• Surfeiting has its costly penalty. Leaders who cannot control their appetite for lack of discipline become its slave, leading to shame.

Proverbs 23:21 (NKJV) For the drunkard and the glutton will come to poverty, and drowsiness will clothe a man with rags.

Committed rising star succeeds

A young leader who was a rising star in his field would remind himself several times a day of his initial commitment and of his responsibility to maintain a diligent attitude; this became the secret of his success.❏

2. Defeat

An independent attitude is self-defeating. It is the outflow of hidden rebellion. Aristotle said, "Inferiors revolt in order that they be equal, and equals that they may be superiors." Sin is basically an act independent of God against God. In Isaiah 14:12-17 (kjv) we read the five "I wills" of Satan that caused his downfall from the highest position in heaven to the lowest state in hell.

1. "I will ascend into heaven":
   Self-assertion.

2. "I will exalt my throne above the stars of God":
   Self-exaltation.

3. "I will sit also upon the mount of the congregation":
   Self-aggrandizement.

4. "I will ascend above the heights of the clouds":
   Self-promotion.

5. "I will be like the Most High":
   Self-equalization.

The fifth "I will" was his strong desire to be equal with God, "I will be like the Most High." Self-promotion for selfish reasons turns to self-demotion. **He who acts independently of God has no power to carry him through life.**

Jesus said in John 15:5 (nkjv), "for without Me you can do nothing." Pride is a head stuffed with self-confidence and is God's greatest enemy in man.

Pride defeats promising young leader

I invited a promising young man to join our operation. He was gifted and had traveled in ministry with favorable results. When he arrived at our office he was nervous, his face was changing colors, and he adamantly and assertively said with a loud voice,

"Unless I am equal with you I will not accept working with you."
I said to him, "We are all equally important to God, but not equally
positioned." He had the opportunity to be trained to become a
worldwide leader, speaking into the lives of thousands of leaders,
but his pride of heart defeated him.❏

Principle	*Comment*
210. Unaccountable leaders are disastrous, for where there is no accountability, there is no restraint.	• The greatest of all human tendencies that hurt leaders most is an independent attitude that acts wildly.

*1 Corinthians 12:12-21 (NKJV)   For as the body is one
and has many members, but all the members of that one
body, being many, are one body, so also is Christ {13}...
{18} But now God has set the members each one of them,
in the body just as He pleased...{19}...{21} And the eye
cannot say to the hand, "I have no need of you"; nor
again the head to the feet, "I have no need of you."*

Principle	*Comment*
211. A transgressing leader will never be able to overcome sin or enjoy a life of being more than a conqueror, for sin corrodes him from within, weakens his will, and contaminates his desires. It renders him helpless.	• To the measure we love God, we hate sin, which is God's greatest enemy and ours. Sin demoralizes character and leads to distraction, ending up in destruction. But thank God who made a way back to His fold through true repentance.

Matthew 26:14-16 (NKJV) Then one of the twelve, called Judas Iscariot, went to the chief priests {15} and said, "What are you willing to give me if I deliver Him to you?" And they counted out to him thirty pieces of silver. {16} So from that time he sought opportunity to betray Him.

---

212. Leaders who underestimate the power and pressure of sin and its consequences, become its victims and suffer greatly.	• Only the power of God can conquer the power of sin through the blood of Christ. Christ within makes us more than conquerors.

Romans 6:16 (NIV) ...you are slaves to the one whom you obey—whether you are slaves to sin, which leads to death, or to obedience, which leads to righteousness?

Principle	*Comment*
213. When a leader's failure is sensationalized without the lesson being learned, it is usually repeated and leads him to a disastrous end.	• Unlearned lessons are often repeated with greater disappointment. Failing to learn from previous failures multiplies them. Continuous failure ends up in defeat.

1 Samuel 15:26-28 (NKJV)   But Samuel said to Saul, "I will not return with you, for you have rejected the word of the LORD, and the LORD has rejected you from being king over Israel." {27} And as Samuel turned around to go away, Saul seized the edge of his robe, and it tore. {28} So Samuel said to him, "The LORD has torn the kingdom of Israel from you today, and has given it to a neighbor of yours, who is better than you."

214. The leader who operates alone will end up alone.	• Where there's no one to lead, no one can be a leader.

Proverbs 12:15 (NKJV)   The way of the fool is right in his own eyes, but he who heeds counsel is wise.

3. Rebellion

Rebellion is an open war of man's will against God's will—setting one's self totally against God's right to rule. We must acknowledge God's creatorship and ownership upon our lives. The accountability of a rebel is the greatest, seeing that it is a defiant and willful act.

Failing to be submissive is the worst degree of rebellion. The further a person moves away from the center of God's will, the harder he becomes toward God and man. Rebellion is a foolish decision that befalls all selfish people who are graduates of the University of Ignorance. He who wants the best for his life submits to God; he who wants the worst rebels, and suffers greatly for it.

Some people excel in rebellion just to be famous, even if it is at the high price of perpetual suffering. Satan finds full expression of his wickedness through rebels who choose to work for him at the cost of their lives.

People who live to submit to God wholeheartedly are those who have discovered and mastered one of the greatest secrets of joyful living.

Hidden rebellion topples leader

A missionary was serving successfully on several mission fields with his family. He was gifted in composing songs and choruses that were a blessing to many. Upon coming back on furlough, his hidden rebellion, which he managed to suppress rather than surrender to God, was manifested. He suddenly left God, his wife, children, and ministry and plunged into acts of open rebellion that devastated his family and caused weak ones to stumble.❏

His new style of life was diametrically opposed to what he believed and had taught others for many years. Hidden seed is bound to grow at the opportune time, when the atmosphere is conducive. It pays to be open with God, in total surrender.

Leaders with an independent spirit suffer from:

- Having a low self-image.
- Having low self-esteem.
- Retaliating for being abused.
- Being in a school with a legalistic environment.
- Being degraded while growing up.
- Having no value of human dignity.
- Venting stored up resentments.
- Having an inflated ego.
- Being overpraised when too young to deserve and take it.
- Having a spirit of rebellion.
- Having pride of heart to show-off.
- Not having been loved genuinely.

Principle	*Comment*
215. When a leader greets the call to accountability with indignation, rather than with submission and devotion, he reveals his inner subtlety and hidden rebellion against the headship of Christ to rule over him.	• Refusing accountability is outright rebellion against the Lordship of Christ. A leader who takes that road opens himself up to the invasion of demons— their influence will compel him to constantly violate God's laws.

Proverbs 1:24-26 (NKJV)   Because I have called and you refused, I have stretched out my hand and no one regarded, {25} because you disdained all my counsel, and would have none of my rebuke, {26} I also will laugh at your calamity; I will mock when your terror comes,

---

216. Some leaders suffer from hardening of the arteries, while unaccountable leaders suffer from hardness of the heart. Many rebellious leaders suffer from both.	• It is safer to be broken before God and to be pliable in His hand. This is the key to prompt obedience in life. Our safety in life lies in our total submission to God.

Exodus 9:7 (NKJV)   Then Pharaoh sent, and indeed, not even one of the livestock of the Israelites was dead. But the heart of Pharaoh became hard, and he did not let the people go.

Principle	**Comment**

217. Lack of accountability in a leader is a dangerous sign of an independent character.

- Hidden rebellion is a menace that manifests itself in independence from God and man.

1 Kings 12:13-15 (NKJV)   Then the king answered the people roughly, and rejected the advice which the elders had given him; {14}...{15} So the king did not listen to the people; for the turn of events was from the LORD, that He might fulfill His word, which the LORD had spoken by Ahijah the Shilonite to Jeroboam the son of Nebat.

218. A counterfeit leader lets problems pile up and allows people freedom to do their own thing and go their own way, unchecked and undisciplined.

- God deliver us from Satan's agents of destruction. Such leaders are most detrimental to society. They cause disaster in every move they make.

Zechariah 11:17 (NKJV)   "Woe to the worthless shepherd, who leaves the flock! A sword shall be against his arm and against his right eye; his arm shall completely wither, and his right eye shall be totally blinded."

4. Abusiveness

No one has any right to oppress or dominate others, regardless of their position. Violating people's rights demeans their dignity and degrades their self-esteem. It insults their Creator.

Abusing others is the misuse of power. Leaders must bring out the best in people. They also must give them their best in order that they may give their best for God in full cooperation. The greatest challenge to leaders is how to use the power constructively by edifying and maturing their people so that they become more productive.

People produce more by being respected and commended than by being despised and harshly commanded. Respecting others is showing them how valuable they are to us. The Bible declares in Psalm 138:6 that God has respect for the lowly.

Leaders who are abusive reveal how cheap and immature they are. Leadership is not domination but liberation so that people can function to their fullest capacity. People are valuable to God and must be led, not driven; they must be fed decisive principles not starved by scolding.

Abusing people shows how small we are while pretending to be great at the expense of hurting others. When people cannot endure any more, it backfires. Samuel Goodrich said, "Abuse is the weapon of the vulgar." The way we treat people reveals exactly what we really are. People always deserve the best treatment from their leaders.

Abusive pastor hinders the Spirit of God

I was attending a meeting where people were exhorted by their pastor to pray for whatever they had on their hearts. The Spirit of the Lord was moving graciously, directing and inspiring individuals in their prayers. Suddenly, while one of them was praying, the pastor didn't like his prayers, interrupted him, and began to critically abuse him. He was injured deeply and so were we. From that moment on, the quenched Spirit of the Lord departed from the meeting and no one dared to pray for fear of being attacked mercilessly.❑

Principle	*Comment*
219. When a leader has an independent spirit, it usually leads to abuses; where there is no account-ability, there's no restraint to his oppressing spirit.	• Oppressors oppress others because they themselves are oppressed. Oppression is the result of giving place to the Devil to wreak havoc in life.

1 Samuel 13:8-15 (NKJV)   Then he waited seven days, according to the time set by Samuel. But Samuel did not come to Gilgal; and the people were scattered from him. {9} So Saul said, "Bring a burnt offering and peace offerings here to me." And he offered the burnt offering. {10}...

Principle	*Comment*
220. A leader who rejects God—the Creator of the universe who sets all standards and divine principles, and governs all its activities and movements—setting himself up as a mini-god, becomes a tyrant over others with no one higher than himself to account to.	• There is a destructive spirit hidden in those who are independent. It is self-destructing and projects destruction that hurts many people unnecessarily. Pride of heart inflates crooked leaders' heads causing them to take the route of self-exaltation.

Daniel 4:29-37 (NKJV) ...{30} The king spoke, saying, "Is not this great Babylon, that I have built for a royal dwelling by my mighty power and for the honor of my majesty?" {31} While the word was still in the king's mouth, a voice fell from heaven: "King Nebuchadnezzar, to you it is spoken: the kingdom has departed from you! {32} And they shall drive you from men."...

- An independent leader is an avowed atheist undercover. He consults no one; he listens to no one; he interacts with no one. No one has any input into his life. He is accountable to no one since he has appointed himself as the supreme authority.

- Such leaders never improve seeing they have no model to look up to but themselves. They are stagnant and lonely. They suffer from the incurable disease, SWT (Sick With Themselves).

V. The Balance

Balance is built on adhering to sound principles through knowledge of ethics and wholesome behavior that shines with honesty and integrity. Extremism is a sign of deception that begins with ignorance and a closed mind, which puts a person in the category of fools. Swinging the pendulum from one extreme to another dissipates the purpose of existence. No one is going to get anything accomplished being an extremist; that usually leads to fanaticism.

An extremist also suffers from an inflated head due to wild guessing in every step he takes. Ignorance and pretense are the costliest things on earth and many are certified club members. They suffer from stiff necks that support heads loaded with compacted hot air.

The arena of safety thrives on the shoulders of leaders who know the pros and cons of life. They are well-read, well-traveled, and well-fed with the best of wisdom which they glean from the wise, those who are resourcefully rich in experiences. They have the capability of weighing people, circumstances, issues, and matters at hand. They pass a balanced judgment based on honest research, unbiased investigation, and wise conclusions.

Leaders who are richly informed make better judgments. The world is suffering from imbalance in every sphere of life. The cry of the masses is, *"Give us balanced leaders who are safe to follow!"*

Imbalance turns board meeting into fist fight

Prejudice marred the judgment of a leader in a serious business meeting. The opposition, fearing his attitude and actions would plunge the company into bankruptcy, spoke out vehemently against him. Tempers flared and the arguments turned to fist fights, ending the meeting. Only as they were exhausted did the raging battle cease.

At the cost of their pride, they agreed to call upon a reputable leader who was known for his wisdom and balanced judgment to handle the case and mediate a reconciliation. He responded as hoped and returned the company to a solid and safe standing. What a price!❑

A. Consider advice from men and counsel from God

The countless blessings we receive from God and the bountiful advice we receive from mature men enrich our lives as we continue to see our constant need for both.

No one was born a self-sufficient entity. We were born a needy people all of our lives, but the Bible assures us in Philippians 4:19 (nkjv) that "...my God shall supply all your need..." Nor were we born learned. Everything we know, God directly taught us by His Spirit, through His Word, or through people more mature than we are. We owe so much to God and to others whom God has used and is still using.

Seeing our constant need for God and for each other helps us to be humbly receptive and seek help. Every counsel of God and wise advice from each other adds valuable enrichment to us that makes us resourceful, enriching others in return. We become vessels of honor indeed.

Beautiful but useless

A lady was passing by a house where there was a rummage sale. A beautiful vessel attracted her attention. The art work, the colors, and the quality of craftsmanship were superb. It was only 25 cents. She bought it without examination or hesitation. When she took it home she had no immediate use for it.

One day she had some friends for a meal and thought of using this lovely vessel. She poured juice in it and set it on the nicely set table. Suddenly she discovered, to her astonishment, a leak from a small crack that was unnoticeable to the eye and only detectable when it was being used.❑

Appearances can be deceiving. It is usefulness that counts most. We all have to watch for any leakage in our lives as we contain the presence and the truth of God. **Nothing cracks a vessel of honor more than the entrance of pride when we become successful and begin to act independently from God and man.**

Principle	*Comment*
221. An accountable leader considers the advice of men, but gets his final counsel from the Spirit of the Lord.	• The wise benefit from both God and man and make perpetual progress. A heart that seeks God never lacks wisdom.

Proverbs 19:21 (NKJV)   There are many plans in a man's heart, nevertheless the Lord's counsel; that will stand.

---

222. If nothing is added or subtracted periodically in the way a leader operates, then nothing is gained in the process of his life and operation. Progress requires it.	• Progress requires addition and subtraction. A sound operation thrives on taking periodic inventories. Self-examination and self-judgment are necessary for progress.

Job 2:10 (NKJV)   But he said to her, "You speak as one of the foolish women speaks. Shall we indeed accept good from God, and shall we not accept adversity?" In all this Job did not sin with his lips.

B. Checks and balances bring safety

It is absolutely imperative that we have the wisdom and experience of others who can safeguard us as we share the things that are dear to our hearts. Who is speaking into your life? How much do you see your need for others? Some self-appointed leaders disqualify themselves by refusing to take orders. They reject counsel, block the avenue of sound suggestions, and finally believe their ideas are final and use no others.

No leader is safe without checks and balances to safeguard his life and his operation. The world will be safer with leaders who see their needs. The less a leader knows about his role the more he thinks he's absolutely right. It is most detrimental to say the least.

Refusal to heed advice leads to leader's demise

A promising leader was gaining worldwide fame when he started to suffer from an inflated ego, swelled head, and enlarged chest. His problems began to loom large when he was confronted regarding reports from different countries that revealed dangerous inconsistencies in his character. When he refused to face these issues, the group with which he was associated revoked his credentials. He refused counsel and took a more independent route that plunged him into deeper problems, which cost him his family, his ministry, and his name.❏

To gain status without gaining stature is very costly as pride usually goes before a fall.

Arrogant chairman loses position

There was a business meeting of a serious nature due to violation of principles. The qualified board members were actively participating in a lively discussion offering valuable, remedial suggestions. The chairman, however, refused all input offered, insisting that he was right and everyone else was wrong. The rest of the board members felt this situation was intolerable. As a result, the chairman's strong independent action brought an end to his career.❑

Woe to any leader who thinks he is always right in his own sight, for he will have much to answer for.

A gesture for safety
Another brother and I were ministering around the world on a long trip. Every time he wrote an article to send to his office for publication in his magazine, he would give it to me to proofread for theological and grammatical correctness. Though he was more capable than I, he was humble enough to ask for safety through checks and balances. I always admired his gesture.❑

None of us are born independent entities sealed with self-sufficiency. Seeing our desperate need for each other keeps us interacting with each other and safeguards us from the pride of our heart.

Principle	*Comment*
223. The leader who abides by the system of checks and balances is safe and safe to follow.	• No one is above accountability but God. Self-made mini-gods think they are God.

Acts 14:27 (NKJV) Now when they [Paul and Barnabas]
had come [to Antioch] and gathered the church together,
they reported all that God had done with them, and that
He had opened the door of faith to the Gentiles.

VI. The Benefits of Being an Accountable Leader

An accountable leader benefits greatly from abiding by the laws of God. He is always aware of the presence of God. He thinks, speaks, and does everything in the light of God's presence. He is free from inhibitions, he has nothing to hide, seeing he walks in the light as God is in the light. His transparency before God and man gives him the great benefit of a clear conscience that triggers his joyful disposition and gains for him the confidence and full cooperation of his followers.

He is proved and pruned by God, and highly regarded by man for his wholesome mannerism and the honest way he conducts his affairs. His fair treatment of all, regardless of their rank and file, endears him to their hearts and brings him their full support. His close walk with God makes him a trusted leader who can be entrusted with the secrets and plans of God for the end time.

He regards God as his daily Judge, as well as his final Judge. Such an attitude helps him walk and enjoy life in the Spirit with all its liberating advantages and abundance of fruit that glorifies God and blesses man. Accountable leaders walk in the fear of God Who enjoys them, and they enjoy Him for time and eternity.

Shamed, broken, and repentant leader given second chance

It was on the eve of Father's Day when a leader discovered a scandal in his operation. He ruled with a rod of iron and was hated by his subordinates. Their morale had reached zero, their cooperation had dwindled down, and the whole operation had come to a halt. Finally, at the family gathering, his embarrassment reached its height. He was furious at the sense of shame and his shattered ego went into a volcanic eruption, spewing its destructive lava on those far and near.

At this point, while the atmosphere was intoxicated by his arrogance, God moved on a visitor, a friend of one of his sons whom he had never met before. The wisdom of God began to flow through him with an irresistible anointing, revealing the plan of God for successful living by surrendering to Him totally and obeying Him explicitly.

The Holy Spirit brought bitter conviction to his heart and a miracle took place as he broke without the ability to control his tears. **He surrendered** and other family members with him as they saw an unbelievable miracle before their eyes. The miserable evening turned to a joyful celebration. This tyrant and unkind leader became a loving, tender person with a mellow spirit. His people were totally affected and his new style of leadership became Christlike. The business thrived greatly and the Lord was glorified.❏

Transformed Lives

It is indeed the inner mysterious working of the grace of God when:

- **Arrogance** turns to *humility*.
- **Dogmatism** turns to *flexibility*.
- **Hardness** turns to *tenderness*.
- **Harshness** turns to *kindness*.

The major operation of the Holy Spirit is transforming lives for the glory of God.

A. Enjoys the confidence and cooperation of his followers

The richest leader is one who has gained the confidence and full cooperation of his people due to walking with God with a heart overflowing with love.

There are three reasons *why people fail to trust their leaders*:
1. They don't really know the heart of their leader; he's a closed personality.
2. They know him well and observe his inconsistencies.
3. He continues to break his promises and disappoint them.

The leader who wins the hearts of his people through serving them well will have their cooperation to the end.

A good leader inspires people to have confidence in themselves and their ability to perform. A great leader inspires people to have confidence in his leadership to lead them on through his proven ability to perform. A godly leader inspires people to put their full confidence in God. This is the exhortation of the Psalmist revealing the central Scripture in the Bible, "It is better to trust in the Lord than to put confidence in man." (Psalm 118:8, kjv)

The key to a leader's long vacation

A leader was on a long vacation which he rightfully deserved as it had accumulated for several years during which he had poured out his utmost strength to build his operation in its formative years. One day while swimming in the pool of his hotel, he met other executives on short vacations who wished they could enjoy a long vacation as he was. One of them asked him some alarming questions, "Aren't you afraid the operation will collapse in your absence? Will the production fall short of the quota? Will a rival take over?" This was his immediate reply: "I enjoy the confidence and cooperation of my people." We always reap to the measure we sow.❏

Dependable leaders are noted for their:

- Faithfulness .... they keep their word.
- Commitment .... they stand fully by their allegiance.
- Sacrifice .... they spare nothing.
- Caring..................... they serve with empathy.
- Loving .... they minister from the heart.
- Reliability .... they carry through their responsibilities.
- Testimony .... they have a disciplined character.
- Competence .... they are well-trained.
- Aggressiveness ...... they move ahead with utmost diligence.
- Consistency .... they enjoy a strong relationship with
  God that makes them stable.

Principle	*Comment*
224. Conscientious leaders operate with the highest integrity before God and man, and they gain the confidence and cooperation of both.	• There's no substitute for transparency; it reveals a clear conscience and peace of mind, coupled with a sweet spirit and a right attitude.

*Genesis 18:17-19 (NKJV) ...{19} "For I [the LORD]
have known him [Abraham], in order that he may
command his children and his household after him,
that they keep the way of the LORD, to do righteousness and justice, that the LORD may bring to Abraham
what He has spoken to him."*

Principle	*Comment*
225. An accountable leader is strong on principles, and he gains the full confidence of his people as they observe his conscientious behavior and ministry before God and man.	• Abiding by divine principles solidifies a leader's position. It keeps him in perfect alignment with the will of God to fulfill His purpose. It brings him up to God's standard with great delight.

Mark 6:18 (NKJV)   For John had said to Herod, "It is not lawful for you to have your brother's wife."

226. The leader who keeps his word and fulfills his promises enjoys the confidence of both friend and foe.	• Confidence is gained when a leader is serious in his commitment to serving others faithfully and diligently.

Matthew 5:33-37 (NIV)   ...{34} "But I tell you, Do not swear at all:...{37} Simply let your 'Yes' be 'Yes,' and your 'No,' 'No'; anything beyond this comes from the evil one."

Principle	*Comment*

227. An accountable leader gains the confidence of his followers because he is faithful and honest in handling the matters entrusted to him.

- What people see in an honest leader they greatly admire. Such leaders have the allegiance and full support of their people.

Acts 20:36-38 (NKJV)   And when he had said these things, he knelt down and prayed with them all. {37} Then they all wept freely, and fell on Paul's neck and kissed him, {38} sorrowing most of all for the words which he spoke, that they would see his face no more. And they accompanied him to the ship.

228. Only faithful leaders who are men of their word can be trusted by God and man.

- He who keeps his word must back it up with his life. It is costly to be faithful.

James 5:12 (NKJV)   But above all, my brethren, do not swear, either by heaven or by earth or with any other oath. But let your "Yes," be "Yes," and your "No," "No," lest you fall into judgment.

Principle	*Comment*
229. A leader who is particular about keeping his promises will build up a reputation for being trustworthy, reliable, and a pleasant person to work for.	• He who would enjoy the confidence of others must back up his words by his deeds. Consistent good manners and persistent performance are great assets.

Colossians 4:7-8 (NKJV) Tychicus, a beloved brother, faithful minister, and fellow servant in the Lord, will tell you all the news about me. {8} I am sending him to you for this very purpose, that he may know your circumstances and comfort your hearts,

---

230. The dependable leader is a great asset to the people who place their confidence in him, for he always keeps his word.	• Accountability requires the greatest measure of discipline on a constant basis. Discipline must be systematic to be effective.

Acts 18:21 (NKJV) but [Paul] took leave of them, saying, "I must by all means keep this coming feast in Jerusalem; but I will return again to you, God willing." And he sailed from Ephesus.

B. Enjoys life

Leaders who enjoy God enjoy life with all its possibilities and rewards. Leaders whose supreme joy is the Lord become His delight indeed. There is mutual enjoyment that cannot be abated due to strong mutual commitment. Jesus, our example, declared in John 8:29 (nkjv), "...I always do those things that please Him." The Father in turn says of Him in Matthew 3:17 (nkjv), "This is My beloved Son, in whom I am well pleased."

The height of enjoyment in life is in expressing utmost appreciation for the Giver of life, Who sustains it perfectly and protects it by His power.

A recipe for joyful living

A leader was asked the reason for his exuberant disposition. He replied, "I am always conscious of God's indwelling presence. I am possessed by my Creator Who gave me a grateful heart, a praising tongue, and a worshipful spirit. He has all of me. He is all in all to me."❏

There are *three kinds of people:*
1. Those whose happiness depends on what happens.

2. Those who have spurts of joy once in a while.

3. Those who enjoy having a joyful disposition through having a strong relationship with the Lord, which sensitizes their spirit to His Spirit. Psalm 16:11 (nkjv) says, "...in Your presence is fullness of joy; at Your right hand are pleasures forevermore."

Principle	*Comment*
231. Accountable leaders find meaning in life, and they enjoy every moment of it.	• They live for God's ultimate and are not hindered by the time and means it takes to reach it to please Him.

Proverbs 8:30 (NKJV) ...I was daily His delight, rejoicing always before Him.

---

232. Accountable leaders appreciate life and welcome its responsibilities with joy.	• A grateful heart overflows with joyful appreciation due to a sense of indebtedness to God.

Psalms 104:33 (NKJV) I will sing to the LORD as long as I live; I will sing praise to my God while I have my being.

---

233. Accountable leaders are full of vigor and vitality.	• Basking in the presence of God revitalizes a leader with God's extras.

Deuteronomy 34:7 (NKJV) Moses was one hundred and twenty years old when he died. His eyes were not dim nor his natural vigor diminished.

Principle	*Comment*

234. Accountable leaders look younger than their age.

- They are free from fear and worry owing to their honesty.

1 Samuel 16:11-12 (NKJV)   And Samuel said to Jesse, "Are all the young men here?" Then he said, "There remains yet the youngest, and there he is, keeping the sheep." And Samuel said to Jesse, "Send and bring him. For we will not sit down till he comes here." {12} So he sent and brought him in. Now he was ruddy, with bright eyes, and good-looking. And the LORD said, "Arise, anoint him; for this is the one!"

235. Accountable leaders seem to maintain their youth because of their diligence in performance.

- The freedom of a clear conscience constantly rejuvenates a leader. It continually revives him.

Acts 24:16 (NKJV)   "This being so, I myself always strive to have a conscience without offense toward God and men."

Conscience clear? Have no fear!

A *guilty conscience* is the heaviest load to carry:

- It *oppresses* the soul.
- It *darkens* the mind.
- It *quenches* the spirit.
- It *convicts* the heart.
- It *tortures* the emotions.
- It *upsets* the function of the glands.
- It *wears out* the nervous system.
- It *disturbs* the function of the digestive system.
- It *depletes* the energy of the body.
- It *ages* people faster, during the duration of their guilt, until it is cleared through repentance.

God has given us:
- The *spirit of power* to overcome demonic forces.
- The *spirit of love* to overcome people's hatred.
- The *spirit of a sound mind* to overcome problems.

C. Overcomes difficulties and mistakes

Leaders who submit to the Lordship of Christ, master life with all its difficulties and failures. Submission releases fresh anointing and power to overcome.

Nothing is difficult to the diligent while everything is difficult to the lazy. Difficulties are things we have not known or tackled before until we master them. Difficulties help us grow stronger in our determination to overcome. Why be "undercomers" overcome by difficulties when we can be overcomers right on the top of everything? Some difficulties are imaginary while others are real, challenging us to rise and seek God's wisdom for the answer. Difficulties can be either tombstones under which we are buried or stepping stones for our promotion. Our attitude determines which it will be.

More than conquerors

I have a missionary friend who is a jack-of-many-trades and a master of them all. He never backs down from any challenge that crosses his path. He lives in the jungles of Africa about 400 miles from the nearest city. He preaches, builds churches, rebuilds broken bridges, and repairs cars. His wife doctors the sick, combating all kinds of sicknesses and diseases. The stories they tell of what they have gone through are out of this world and would discourage most people. They are indeed more than conquerors through Christ Who divinely enables them.❏

There are *three kinds of people:*
1. The **Comers**—They are passive, negative, easily influenced by the environment, and flow with the crowd.
2. The **Undercomers**—They live in fear that paralyzes their faith and renders their faculties powerless. They surrender

easily due to having no inner resistance. They live under their privileges.

3. The **Overcomers**—They are determined winners in their hearts and subdue everything that stands in their way that would hinder them from reaching their goals. They specialize in tackling the impossible.

Principle	*Comment*
236. An experienced leader masters the most difficult moves in life without being affected by them.	• Rich experiences help leaders sail smoothly on rough seas. They give them assurance of success.

Romans 8:38-39 (NKJV)   For I am persuaded that neither death nor life, nor angels nor principalities nor powers, nor things present nor things to come, {39} nor height nor depth, nor any other created thing, shall be able to separate us from the love of God which is in Christ Jesus our Lord.

---

237. An accountable leader who loves God masters all fears in life.	• Divine consciousness frees us from all fear and inhibition.

2 Timothy 1:7 (NKJV)   For God has not given us a spirit of fear, but of power and of love and of a sound mind.

Principle	*Comment*

238. The leader who sees himself as others see him easily mends his ways and makes a speedy recovery.

- As we need mirrors daily, so we need others to see for us our blind spots that mar the image of Christ and retard progress.

Hebrews 3:13 (NKJV)   ...but exhort one another daily, while it is called "Today," lest any of you be hardened through the deceitfulness of sin.

---

239. In some cases, the contributions of leaders outweigh their mistakes and help them survive an ordeal. But only if they rectify their mistakes and learn the valuable lessons will they make strides in their own personal development.

- Mistakes teach us how not to do it, if we are disciplined enough. Some successful leaders attribute their success to learning from their costly failures that awakened in them a sense of serious-ness, coupled with daily discipline and alertness.

Psalms 51:1-19 (NKJV)   Have mercy upon me, O God {2} Wash me thoroughly from my iniquity, and cleanse me from my sin. {3} For I acknowledge my transgressions, and my sin is always before me. {4} Against You, You only, have I sinned. {5}...{10} Create in me a clean heart, O God, and renew a steadfast spirit within me...{13} Then I will teach transgressors Your ways, and sinners shall be converted to You....

D. Is an intimate friend of God

Friendship with God fortifies a leader's character and gives him the courage to face life with boldness of faith.

In James 4:8, the apostle of practical Christianity exhorts the earnest and sincere who desire to enjoy the best of life on earth to get close to God and He will get close to them. Definitely this supreme desire is born of God and brings the greatest pleasure to His heart. Following God from afar dries the bones and dampens one's spirit, culminating in the loss of interest of the things of God. No wonder the psalmist exclaimed, "It is good for me to draw near to God." (Psalm 73:28, nkjv)

The closer we draw to God, the more we experience His sweet presence and calming peace quieting our souls. We enjoy the fresh air of gladness and a continual surge of His divine power that makes His life a living reality, causing us to sing, "Heaven came down and glory filled my soul." It is vain trying to describe what happens to a soul that enjoys intimacy with God. Human vocabulary fails to unfold all the dynamism that surges into one's spirit as the flood lights of eternity beam and penetrate into the depth of the inner man. Man becomes speechless for loss of words to describe in human terms all the divine sensations that need a heavenly vocabulary to express.

Suicidal leader finds God afresh through old friend

An unstable leader who was greatly gifted in ministry but bankrupt in character was driven to despair and decided to end his life. He could not bear the continual ups and downs. His inconsistencies tormented him. It was on his way to the ocean to drown himself that he met an old friend that he had not seen for many years. It was well declared that *our **extremity** brings God's **opportunity***. While each was inquiring of the other his whereabouts, this suicidal leader discovered that his old friend lived alone in a secluded area after his family members grew up and left the nest. He sensed an aroma and a sweet breath of God while with him.

Out of the heart of his old friend began to flow fresh prophetic revelation unveiling the secrets of God for the end time. It excited him and renewed his interest to live as close to God as his old friend. He took a sabbatical from his responsibilities and lived with his friend and learned the secret and blessing of divine intimacy with God. The call of God upon his life beckoned him to return as a new man who lives in the presence of God and who speaks out of the heart of God.❑

Principle	*Comment*
240. An accountable leader, though he fears God, is not afraid of Him because they are intimate friends.	• Closeness to God destroys one's fear of man. It contributes toward inner stability and steadfast-ness in walking with God.

Exodus 20:21 (NKJV)   So the people stood afar off, but Moses drew near the thick darkness where God was.

Divine Intimacy

- Cures all fears and inner complexities.
- Cures all confusion and inner conflicts.
- Cures all misconceptions and deceptions.
- Cures all doubts and unbelief.
- Develops full assurance of faith.
- Develops inner calmness.
- Develops mutually healthy relationships.

E. Is restrained from evil

An accountable leader does everything in life while keeping an eye on the judgment seat of Christ.

It is this consciousness of God's presence that restrains us from evil and helps us to focus our eyes and interests on the Lord as He becomes more real, near, and dear to our hearts.

Leader saved from the brink of destruction

A leader whose life and ministry were flourishing greatly suddenly fell to depth of sin at an "unguarded moment." In his despair he lost all desire to serve God out of a sense of conviction and shame. His condition was kept private but fear of being discovered gripped his heart and tortured him until it became unbearable.

He had to make a quick decision as to which way to turn. After pondering the matter seriously, he decided to take a few days off and go to a Christian retreat and seek the Lord. Upon arrival at his room he found a large print Bible open to Psalm 139 (See Appendix C). He sat on the floor and began to weep remorsefully with much pain in his heart.

His eyes were fixed on the psalm. When he was able to control himself and regain his composure, he began to read loudly and slowly enough to hear the cry of the psalmist. Suddenly he had a revelation of the awesomeness of God as the Omniscient, Omnipresent, and Omnipotent One.

His true repentance brought restoration of joy and liberty beyond his past experiences. He began to be more enthused about walking with God than serving Him. From that day on, he served God, fully aware of the presence of God Who sees him, Who hears him, and Who is fully aware of all of his movements. He became more effective and fruitful than in the past.❏

Principle	*Comment*
241. Accountability in leadership brings restraint from evil and makes a leader answerable for every move and decision he makes. It puts a check on his behavior and his relationships with God and man.	• Without accountability there is no safety, nor will there be any fruitfulness. Accountability calms the emotions and helps leaders walk uprightly in their pursuit to serve God. It makes us aware of His presence.

Proverbs 1:32-33 (NKJV) "For the turning away of the simple will slay them, and the complacency of fools will destroy them; {33} but whoever listens to me will dwell safely, and will be secure, without fear of evil."

---

242. The leader who is under authority is restrained from doing evil because he is faced with accountability on a constant basis.	• Submission to higher authority saves a leader from the disaster that befalls rebels. Wholehearted submission is the key to peace and safety.

Romans 13:3-4 (NKJV) For rulers are not a terror to good works, but to evil. Do you want to be unafraid of the authority? Do what is good, and you will have praise from the same. {4} For he is God's minister to you for good. But if you do evil, be afraid; for he does not bear the sword in vain; for he is God's minister, an avenger to execute wrath on him who practices evil.

Principle	**Comment**
243. Most leaders who exercise unlimited power become corrupt and abased because they have no authority over them to guard them for their safety.	• Every authority has boundaries that must be regarded. Violating set boundaries mars our relationships with God and man. It is the road to ultimate destruction.

Daniel 4:30-37 (NKJV)   The king spoke, saying, "Is not this great Babylon, that I have built for a royal dwelling by my mighty power and for the honor of my majesty?" {31} While the word was still in the king's mouth, a voice fell from heaven: "King Nebuchadnezzar, to you it is spoken: the kingdom has departed from you..." {33} That very hour the word was fulfilled concerning Nebuchadnezzar...

- The boundaries of the authority of leaders are not limitless. They are delegated by God to be exercised under His supreme authority for the sole fulfillment of His eternal purpose.

- All authority must have guidelines as well as guard-lines that determine the extent of its responsibility and accountability.

F. Is protected

A leader's integrity protects him from the many pitfalls that befall him along the path of his responsibility.

"The integrity of the righteous preserves him." (Psalm 25:21, nkjv) He is galvanized by God's presence and lives and moves in the Spirit who directs his path. The quality of his character is a testimony to the inner working of the grace of God. All accusations hurled against him are futile, and all upheavals that rise to defame him soon come to an end, because his life shines brighter as he exhibits Christlikeness.

Wrongly accused leader relies on God for vindication

Due to jealousy, a leader who was excelling in his ministry was being accused of illicit acts, which he knew nothing about. His accuser insisted on defaming him. There was no retaliation on his part; he forgave and prayed for his accuser who continued to tell a series of lies. He left the matter in the hands of the Lord and continued to shine until his opponent was put to shame by his lawfulness, integrity, and consistency.❑

- *David said* in Psalm 25:21 (nkjv), *"Let integrity and uprightness preserve me,..."*
- *Job said* in Job 27:5 (nkjv), *"...till I die I will not put away my integrity from me."*
- *Solomon said* in Proverbs 11:3 (nkjv), *"The integrity of the upright will guide them,..."*
- *Solomon said* in Proverbs 20:7 (nkjv), *"The righteous man walks in his integrity;..."*
- *Webster's Dictionary says*, *"Integrity is the quality of being of sound moral principle."*

Principle	*Comment*
244. The most protected leader is one who takes his accountability to God and the direct authority over him very seriously.	• Herein lies absolute safety. Submissive leaders gain the favor of God and the confidence of man. They are a joy to work with.

Exodus 4:15-16 (NKJV) *"Now you shall speak to him and put the words in his mouth. And I will be with your mouth and with his mouth, and I will teach you what you shall do. {16} So he shall be your spokesman to the people. And he himself shall be as a mouth for you, and you shall be to him as God."*

---

245. Accountable leaders who walk uprightly are saved from many pitfalls and humiliation.	• Seriousness with God is a great saving factor from the pitfalls that afflict rebellious leaders.

2 Timothy 2:15 (NKJV) *Be diligent to present yourself approved to God, a worker who does not need to be ashamed, rightly dividing the word of truth.*

Principle	*Comment*

246. Leaders who are guided by mature brethren will be saved from the pitfalls of independence. *"But woe to him who is alone when he falls, for he has no one to help him up."* (Eccl. 4:10, nkjv)

- A separated coal loses its fire and becomes useless ash that serves no purpose. Thank God for brethren who can save us from unwarranted trouble through their counsel.

Proverbs 11:14 (NKJV)   Where there is no counsel, the people fall; but in the multitude of counselors there is safety.

---

247. Accountable leaders don't suffer from delay or haste.

- Balance characterizes the lives of accountable leaders.

Proverbs 19:2 (NIV)   It is not good to have zeal without knowledge, nor to be hasty and miss the way.

- The most beneficial counsel is only as good as the use we make of it.
- The better the counsel the more it costs to get it and apply it.
- Counsel ignored is more costly than counsel applied.
- Wise counsel is one of the greatest saving factors in life when heeded before and after it is needed.

G. Is free

When truth finds fulfillment in the life of a leader, it sets him free from bondage and limitations and enables him to fulfill his mission successfully. True freedom is the ability to will with the will of God and find divine enablement to sustain a leader in the process. Only a liberated leader frees his people to be themselves, allowing them to develop while overlooking their weakness. He overcomes their reluctance (due to imbedded fear) to help free them from their inward focus (which causes perplexities and hesitancy) to move forward in harmony. *He is a liberator indeed.*

Leader's joy draws a crowd

A leader was administering certain courses in a general conference with such a freedom and joy that it rallied most of the people to his class. When questioned about his extraordinary joyful disposition he answered, "I walk uprightly before God and man. I have nothing to hide because I live in the light of God's truth that 'will set you free.' (John 8:32, niv)"❑

- **Spiritual freedom** is enjoyed when we **identify** with the truth.
- **Intellectual freedom** is enjoyed when we **believe** the truth.
- **Emotional freedom** is enjoyed when we **imbibe** the truth.
- **Physical freedom** is enjoyed when we **obey** the truth.
- **Experiential freedom** is enjoyed when we **apply** the truth.

Principle	*Comment*

248. Accountable leaders who accept Christ's Lordship over their lives are free from the bondage of habits and secret sins that hamper their progress and bring on the judgment of God.

- Submission to Christ's Lordship gives Him control over all areas of our lives. Submissive leaders enjoy the best of what God bestows upon all who obey Him. They will revel in His abundance.

Hebrews 12:1 (NKJV) Therefore we also, since we are surrounded by so great a cloud of witnesses, let us lay aside every weight, and the sin which so easily ensnares us, and let us run with endurance the race that is set before us,

---

249. Accountable leaders are free from irritability, knowing that it puts them in reverse gear and hinders their progress.

- Learning to be patient with ourselves and others frees us from ill-feelings and nervous breakdowns which are detrimental.

1 Thessalonians 5:14 (NKJV) Now we exhort you, brethren, warn those who are unruly, comfort the faint-hearted, uphold the weak, be patient with all.

Principle	*Comment*
250. When a leader is doing the right thing according to God he does not have anything to hide.	• Walking in the light safeguards a leader from hypocritical living and frees his spirit to fulfill God's will.

Genesis 4:9-10 (NKJV) Then the LORD said to Cain, "Where is Abel your brother?" He said, "I do not know. Am I my brother's keeper?" {10} And He said, "What have you done? The voice of your brother's blood cries out to Me from the ground."

The Final Judgment

- Facing God on Judgment Day is the most awesome, inevitable reality in life.
- To some, it will be their greatest joy, due to loving God abundantly, serving Him diligently, and keeping their promises faithfully.
- To others, it will be a humiliating confrontation that will reveal bitter regrets because they loved themselves more than they loved God; did their own thing rather than God's will; lived for selfish pleasure rather than to please God; lived a life of laziness, carelessness, negligence, pride, and rebellion.
- It is the final judgment that really counts most. No *smarty* will escape his turn or evade his sentence.
- We should always live conscious of our accountability before the Judgment Seat of Christ.

Appendix A
Scripture References Used

The following Scripture references are used in this book. The numbers in *italics are principle numbers*, and the numbers in **bold are page numbers** of Scriptures used in introductory text.

Genesis 3:11-13 *181*
Genesis 4:4-5 *14*
Genesis 4:9-10 *250*
Genesis 4:13-14 *173*
Genesis 16:1-5 **99**
Genesis 18:17-19 *224*
Genesis 26:6-10 *164*
Genesis 39:21-23 *100*
Genesis 42:18 *8*
Exodus 3:10 *25*
Exodus 4:15-16 *244*
Exodus 5:2 *171*
Exodus 8:8-15 *194*
Exodus 8:19 *160*
Exodus 9:7 *216*
Exodus 18:13-24 *80*
Exodus 18:17-26 *37*
Exodus 18:25-26 *60*
Exodus 20:21 *240*
Exodus 32:21-26 *180*
Exodus 40:16 *51*
Numbers 13:30-31 *98*
Numbers 20:7-12 *116*
Numbers 32:10-12 *88*
Numbers 32:23 *13, 166,* **2**
Deuteronomy 6:17 *95*
Deuteronomy 11:26-28 **151**
Deuteronomy 31:7-9 *58*
Deuteronomy 34:7 *233*

Joshua 5:13-15 *4*
Joshua 7:19 *53*
Joshua 9:3-27 *172*
Joshua 14:12-14 *135*
Joshua 24:15 *56*
Judges 8:1-3 *200*
1 Samuel 2:12,22-25 *30*
1 Samuel 2:12-18 *107*
1 Samuel 2:12-24 *195*
1 Samuel 3:11-14 *191*
1 Samuel 13:1-15 *176*
1 Samuel 13:8-15 *219*
1 Samuel 13:13-14 *149*
1 Samuel 15:22-23 *182*
1 Samuel 15:26-28 *213*
1 Samuel 16:11-12 *234*
1 Samuel 18:8-9 *48*
1 Samuel 18:16 *26*
2 Samuel 12:1-25 *199*
1 Kings 1:5-14 *108*
1 Kings 3:4-6 *66*
1 Kings 8:56 *94*
1 Kings 12:6-16 *183*
1 Kings 12:13-15 *217*
1 Kings 12:16 *39*
1 Kings 13:33 *196*
1 Kings 14:7-10 *187*
2 Kings 6:13-17 *120*
2 Kings 12:15 **32**

Appendix B
Other Book Titles

The following book titles are being developed or are *in print*:

1. *The Accountable Leader**
2. The Accurate Leader
3. The Affectionate Leader
4. The Assuring Leader
5. The Alert Leader
6. The Amiable Leader
7. The Anointed Leader
8. The Apostolic Leader
9. The Appreciative Leader
10. The Ardent Leader
11. The Assuring Leader
12. The Attentive Leader
13. The Authoritative Leader
14. The Balanced Leader
15. The Challenging Leader
16. The Charismatic Leader
17. The Charitable Leader
18. The Committed Leader
19. The Communicating Leader
20. The Compassionate Leader
21. The Concerned Leader
22. The Conscientious Leader
23. The Consecrated Leader
24. The Consistent Leader
25. The Contented Leader
26. The Courageous Leader
27. The Daring Leader
28. The Decisive Leader
29. The Dedicated Leader
30. The Dependable Leader
31. The Determined Leader
32. The Devoted Leader
33. The Diligent Leader
34. The Discerning Leader
35. The Disciplined Leader
36. The Earnest Leader
37. The Efficient Leader
38. The Eloquent Leader
39. The Encouraging Leader
40. The Enduring Leader
41. The Energizing Leader
42. The Enthusiastic Leader
43. The Ethical Leader
44. The Evangelistic Leader
45. The Excellent Leader
46. *The Exemplary Leader**
47. The Experienced Leader
48. The Faithful Leader
49. The Faith-ful Leader
50. The Fatherly Leader
51. The Fervent Leader
52. The Flexible Leader
53. The Forgiving Leader
54. The Forthright Leader
55. The Friendly Leader
56. The Generous Leader
57. The Goal-Oriented Leader
58. The Godly Leader
59. The Gracious Leader
60. The Healthy Leader
61. The Honest Leader
62. The Honorable Leader
63. The Humble Leader

64. The Industrious Leader
65. The Innovative Leader
66. The Inspiring Leader
67. The Intercessory Leader
68. The Joyful Leader
69. The Just Leader
70. The Kind Leader
71. The Knowledgeable Leader
72. The Leader of Leaders
73. The Leader with Vision
74. The Liberated Leader
75. The Loving Leader
76. The Loyal Leader
77. The Married Leader
78. The Mature Leader
79. The Merciful Leader
80. The Modest Leader
81. The Motivated Leader
82. The Negative Leader
83. The Noble Leader
84. The Obedient Leader
85. The Organized Leader
86. The Pastoral Leader
87. The Patient Leader
88. The Peaceful Leader
89. The Persistent Leader
90. The Polite Leader
91. The Potential Leader
92. The Practical Leader
93. The Principled Leader
94. The Progressive Leader
95. The Prophetic Leader
96. The Prudent Leader
97. The Radiant Leader
98. The Realistic Leader
99. The Refined Leader
100. The Respectful Leader
101. The Responsible Leader
102. The Revolutionary Leader
103. The Righteous Leader
104. The Sacrificial Leader
105. The Scholarly Leader
106. The Seasoned Leader
107. The Secure Leader
108. The Serious Leader
109. The Servant Leader
110. The Sincere Leader
111. The Single Leader
112. The Stable Leader
113. The Stalwart Leader
114. The Steadfast Leader
115. The Submissive Leader
116. The Successful Leader
117. The Teaching Leader
118. The Team Leader
119. The Tender Leader
120. The Thorough Leader
121. The Thoughtful Leader
122. The Trustworthy Leader
123. The Understanding Leader
124. The Unifying Leader
125. The Victorious Leader
126. The Wise Leader
127. The Worshipful Leader
128. The Youth Leader

* **Books in print**

Appendix C
Psalm 139

Psalms 139 (NKJV)   O LORD, You have searched me and known me. {2} You know my sitting down and my rising up; You understand my thought afar off. {3} You comprehend my path and my lying down, and are acquainted with all my ways. {4} For there is not a word on my tongue, but behold, O LORD, You know it altogether. {5} You have hedged me behind and before, and laid Your hand upon me. {6} Such knowledge is too wonderful for me; it is high, I cannot attain it.

{7} Where can I go from Your Spirit? Or where can I flee from Your presence? {8} If I ascend into heaven, You are there; if I make my bed in hell, behold, You are there. {9} If I take the wings of the morning, and dwell in the uttermost parts of the sea, {10} even there Your hand shall lead me, and Your right hand shall hold me. {11} If I say, "Surely the darkness shall fall on me," even the night shall be light about me; {12} indeed, the darkness shall not hide from You, but the night shines as the day; the darkness and the light are both alike to You.

{13} For You formed my inward parts; You covered me in my mother's womb. {14} I will praise You, for I am fearfully and wonderfully made; marvelous are Your works, and that my soul knows very well. {15} My frame was not hidden from You, when I was made in secret, and skillfully wrought in the lowest parts of the earth. {16} Your eyes saw my substance, being yet unformed. And in Your book they all were written, the days fashioned for me, when as yet there were none of them.

{17} How precious also are Your thoughts to me, O God! How great is the sum of them! {18} If I should count them, they would be more in number than the sand; when I awake, I am still with You.

{19} Oh, that You would slay the wicked, O God! Depart from me, therefore, you bloodthirsty men. {20} For they speak against You wickedly; Your enemies take Your name in vain. {21} Do I not hate them, O LORD, who hate You? And do I not loathe those who rise up against You? {22} I hate them with perfect hatred; I count them my enemies.

{23} Search me, O God, and know my heart; try me, and know my anxieties; {24} and see if there is any wicked way in me, and lead me in the way everlasting.

Appendix D
Your Decision Now Counts for Eternity

All life on earth has a beginning and an ending except man's life. He was created by God an eternal being to live forever. The longing in man's heart to live longer triggered the scientific research for longevity. So far this has been man's quest, but to no avail. The Bible tells us that God "set eternity in the hearts of men." (Ecclesiastes 3:11, niv) That is why within his heart there's an instinctive longing for immortality.

Ever since man's fall in sin he has suffered greatly from a guilty conscience, an oppressed mind, a restless spirit, and a void that nothing in life can fill.

Man is roaming the globe searching frantically for answers in everything he can find for his dilemma, only to sink deeper in his evil ways. That's why Jesus came to offer

1. **Forgiveness of sin**
   "...in whom we have redemption through His blood, the forgiveness of sins." Colossians 1:14 (nkjv)

2. **Peace with God**
   "Therefore, having been justified by faith, we have peace with God through our Lord Jesus Christ..." Romans 5:1 (nkjv)

3. **Joy unspeakable**
   "...though now ye see him not, yet believing, ye rejoice with joy unspeakable and full of glory:" 1 Peter 1:8 (kjv)

4. **Love that's eternal**
   "The LORD hath appeared of old unto me, saying, Yea, I have loved thee with an everlasting love..." Jeremiah 31:3 (kjv)

5. **Eternal life**
   "And this is the promise that He has promised us; eternal life." 1 John 2:25 (nkjv)

When we accept Christ as our personal Savior and Lord we enjoy abundant life in our relationship with God as we live to obey Him, do His will, and fulfill His eternal purposes.

Accept Him now and enjoy a foretaste of eternity on earth. You can do this by praying this simple prayer:

> ***Lord, I realize I am a sinner and accept You in my life as Savior and Lord. I love you and desire to walk with you all the days of my life.***

If you prayed this prayer, you have become a child of God and His Spirit now lives in you. "Do you not know that you are the temple of God and that the Spirit of God dwells in you?" 1 Corinthians 3:16 (nkjv).

To grow in your relationship with God and to learn His ways:

1. Read and obey God's Word daily (The Holy Bible)
"Let the word of Christ dwell in you richly..."
Colossians 3:16 (nkjv)

2. Pray to Him
"Then He spoke a parable to them, that men always ought to pray and not lose heart..."   Luke 18:1 (nkjv)

3. Fellowship with other Christians
"And they continued steadfastly in the apostles' doctrine and fellowship..."   Acts 2:42 (nkjv)

4. Tell others what God has done for you and for them
"And we have seen and testify that the Father has sent the Son as Savior of the world."   1 John 4:14 (nkjv)

As you grow in your relationship and knowledge of God, His Spirit will be working in you to make you like Christ, the ultimate example.

Notes

Notes

Notes

Notes

Notes

Notes

Notes

Notes

Notes

Notes

Notes

Notes

Notes

Notes